Free Spirit

A SPIRITUAL MANUAL FOR THE MILLENNIUM
PART 2

by Virginia Swann

The Spiritual Pathway — it's easy at the beginning...

FANTINE PRESS

First published 2006
by
Fantine Press
The Coach House
Stansted Hall
Stansted
Essex CM24 8UD

© 2006 Virginia Swann

The moral rights of the author have been asserted.
All rights reserved in accordance with the
Copyright, Designs and Patents Act, 1988

ISBN 10: 1 901958 09 4
ISBN 13: 978 1 901958 09 6

> Front cover is a portrait of *Sunshine*, one of
> the spirit inspirers who help Virginia.
> Please see page 55

Produced in England by Booksprint

Contents

	Introduction	5
	The Spiritual Pathway	6
	The Freedom of Spirit	7
	What is True Freedom?	8
Chapter 1	What and Where is my Spirit?	11
Chapter 2	The Spiritual Pathway	15
Chapter 3	Signs and Symbols—to Show the Way	29
Chapter 4	Where Am I on the Pathway?	45
Chapter 5	Treading the Pathway	69
Chapter 6	Leaving the Physical Vibration	81
Chapter 7	Life as a Free Spirit	97

Introduction

MY first book "Wish You Were Here?" gave a brief outline of my life and the growth of my spiritual activity. It also covered meditation, the transition from the physical world to the world of spirit, the spheres of life in spirit, spiritual healing and some comments on the structure of planets and the universe.

This book contains information about spiritual development, with personal examples of following the spiritual pathway in life. It shows the increasing difference this choice makes to the life of the person.

The relation of the spiritual pathway to the spheres of spirit life is explained, as progress on the pathway links the person more and more with spirit whilst still living a physical life.

Although guidance and opportunities were given to me continually, the choice to tread the spiritual pathway was always a personal decision.

The explanation of life in the spheres further away from the earth, and how progress is made, was received through meditation, channelling and by astral projection when asleep.

> *Dedicated to my husband,*
> *whose love, support and encouragement*
> *made this book possible.*

The Spiritual Pathway

How hard it is, indeed, to see
And follow the footsteps of the Masters
Strive to be pure in thought, and free
And listen to the voices of the Masters

To seek the cleansing air to breathe
And smell the garden scents of heaven
To choose good food your soul to feed
And taste the living fruits of heaven

To gently touch the pain of others
And feel the healing of your own
To sow kind seeds of love for all your brothers
And reap the harvest of the love you've shown

To stand at last upon the shores of Heaven
To see and hear and feel with spiritual joy
The love of those who trod the path before you
And long have served in God's employ.

The Freedom of Spirit

SPIRIT is always free.

That essence of life in all things, which scientists see as pulsating energy, within the structure of matter, is always moving, living, being.

You cannot "free" your spirit as such, because your spiritual being cannot be bound. You can only realise that you are a free spirit, and your life lived through the material body a temporary expression, and great restriction, of your true reality.

The real you is part of the creative force of life, as is the spiritual reality of all life: in the rocks, the vegetation and the many animals, birds and fish.

Therefore you are forever alive and forever free.

What is True Freedom?

FREEDOM has great importance to the human race; it is often what we strive for—but what is true freedom? Freedom of the body is not freedom of the mind, and restriction of the body is not necessarily restriction of the mind. There is an old saying: "Two men looked out of bars—one saw mud, the other saw stars." We gain freedom by aspiration, by looking upwards rather than downwards, by choosing optimism rather than pessimism, by freeing the mind to consider all possibilities—an open mind is a free mind.

We become the free spirit that we are by forgiving ourselves, and others, for past and present mistakes—this sets us free to begin anew each day.

To do this we have to use our free will, in a positive and loving way, and not the will of other people. Free will, our freedom of choice, is one of the most, if not the most, precious gifts that we possess.

This realisation of the freedom that should be ours is gained by living within the spiritual laws of life, by accepting responsibility, and by rising above and controlling our own nature.

You cannot take freedom because spiritual law governs all life. We see the natural laws of life in operation all the time. These laws govern us all and operate not only at the physical level but for the other vibrations of life also.

If you take your freedom from a certain situation, for example, there will be consequences of your actions that will affect your life and others' lives.

I was introduced to this concept by my brother, who has always understood the importance of free will for individual progression. However, he is older than I am and I will never forget the day we discussed the importance of being able to do what you wished. He told me that one hard fact I should always remember—you could do what you liked, sure enough...and then accept the consequences! You can only grow into the freedom you have earned by your attunement to an expanded expression of life. This entails learning self-control and considering the consequences of your actions, speech and thoughts before you proceed. This sets you free from the demands of your body and the attitude of mind that self-interest is of prime importance. You begin to take a wider view of life that takes into account the needs of others, and to accept that their interests and viewpoints are as valid and important as your own.

In this way, you begin to grow away from the smaller version of yourself towards your higher realities. When you strive to reach your higher aspirations in behaviour and thought this gradual, continuing process has begun. The choice to find this freedom, and the many experiences and changes this choice entails, is the choice to follow what is commonly called "The Spiritual Pathway."

Chapter 1

What and Where is My Spirit?

YOU are your spirit.

To embark on the spiritual pathway of life will take you away from a life centred on the physical world, and bring you to an understanding of your spiritual reality—that you are not a body, but a spirit controlling a body.

Your body is similar to a car, fuelled, controlled and used by you, a spiritual being. You use the body in order to link to, and have an existence in, the physical world in order to gain valuable experience and to grow as a person.

Your body is made up of the raw materials of the world, carbon, water, and so on, just as the flowers, the trees, the rocks, the air and the animal kingdom are made up of these same raw materials. Your body, and, indeed, the whole of the physical universe, is held together by points of energy. This truth has been discovered by scientists as they have delved deeper into the structure of the atoms of life. This is the energy, the power of life, which is used by you, as a spirit, to animate the physical body.

When this energy is withdrawn, the body disintegrates into the raw materials, which return to the earth. This power or energy, which holds the physical universe together, streams from the source of life, that we call so many different names according to our beliefs. It is the power of spirit, the power of life, the "life force."

You are equipped with the energy or power to control your body with your mind, through the mechanism of the brain. The brain can be likened to the most wonderful computer ever made, controlling and organising the body.

The mind is your tool to register your thoughts, to bring about your actions, to impress your will onto the material world, using the brain. Your senses provide you with information about the world, and you act and react in accordance with your desires, intentions and character.

All life is spiritual: the physical world, the physical universe is only a covering held together by these points of energy. So you are always a spiritual being, with several coverings to enable you to be aware of different vibrations of life.

The physical covering in fact restricts the mind to receiving a very limited set of three-dimensional information. Our real selves, our spirits, are always striving to be free of this restriction through our minds, using scientific discoveries, music, art, literature and religion. We contact the experiences of other people in these areas. We begin our own journey from second-hand to first-hand experience when we decide to contribute our own efforts, and start to learn to become creative ourselves.

We have to come to the realisation that although the earthly world has a reality for us, it is truly a façade that is not a permanent reality. Our senses give us a limited and distorted picture of the physical world, and also the life we live is one of constructed inventions of our minds. Gold has no value, for example, in reality. Our titles and positions due to material wealth and power are meaningless when measured against our health and happiness, and that of the people we love.

We often only fully realise the temporary state of the physical when illness occurs, or the death of someone close to us, and yet we see the progression of people from birth to the death of the physical body around us daily.

The oneness of life

All life is one; there are only these different vibrations. We are aware of this in the physical world if we think about it. We know we can only experience a small part of the physical world even; we know that our five senses have their limitations.

We are also aware that our thoughts and feelings are real, and so must have vibrations of existence. To give is to receive because of the inter-relation of all life, whatever we give to life we give to ourselves. We cannot love without putting our mind on the love vibration, and therefore being "tuned in" to receive love. Therefore, we cannot hate without putting our mind on that vibration also. The same applies to fear, depression, happiness, peace and so on.

We have to understand that we need to receive as well as give. We learn to treat others as we would wish to be treated, and that the behaviour that seems perfectly reasonable when it is ours, is not so reasonable when other people behave in exactly the same way to us.

We need to tune in to a more loving and forgiving vibration of life, accepting that happiness and sorrow are two sides of the same coin and that to block emotional contact with others is not a successful way forward. This, of course, takes a lot of courage, and does not mean that you should accept bad treatment or attitudes from other people. The lesson is to not give hate in return for hate, as this does not solve the problem.

We can have no life without each other and without all the other components of our world; we are all interdependent. This is true of our physical life and is true of the mental, emotional and spiritual parts of our lives also. There is no physical life if there is no life force of creative power: there is always thought first and action afterwards.

So it is true to say that there are really no clear-cut divisions between the vibrations of life; all is a blending from one to the other. To reach another vibration of life is a question of tuning in to that vibration. Just as there are instruments that compensate for the limitations of the physical senses, such as infrared cameras, so there are techniques to assist you to tune in to the higher levels of life. Meditation is one of the most helpful techniques as it quietens the physical or "body" section of the mind, and lets the person become aware of higher mental and spiritual vibrations. (There is a chapter on meditation in "Wish You Were Here?")

You become more and more aware of your freedom when you realise that true freedom is not a physical state, but is of the mind. Physical freedom can only be limited and temporary because the physical body is only limited and temporary. When you wish to experience freedom of the mind, which is the first step to experiencing the freedom of your spirit, you are asking to be given the opportunity to choose the spiritual pathway.

Chapter 2

The Spiritual Pathway

THIS spiritual pathway is an exploration of one's own nature, one's own strengths and weaknesses, and your relationships with others. It is an individual journey, because we are all different, and learn in our own way and at our own speed.

As you journey on, it becomes more and more apparent that you need to discard the past, that there are beliefs, attitudes and habits that you need to alter. This is always achieved by a process of theory and practice, as we have to realise that something needs to be done before we can do it!

The most difficult part of this process is not relinquishing places and indeed people, although these are both hard enough. The most painful part is letting go of parts of yourself. We have to learn to leave the "old me" in the past and travel on. This has to be done with love, the importance of loving yourself has to be understood, and put into practice, because you never truly let go of anything on a vibration of hate or dislike.

It is extremely difficult to "forgive and forget," and again, harder to apply this to your own mistakes than those of other people, although the two are intertwined.

However, there is another well-known saying that "when the student is ready the teacher appears." The guidance needed as you tread this pathway is always provided, sometimes directly from spirit, sometimes through spirit people who still possess a body—we are all spirit.

It is important to realise that we are all always spirit, and the physical body can be likened to an overcoat that we have put on in order to tolerate the "bad weather," the heavy vibration, of the physical world.

This also applies to the lower vibrations of our mind, and we will be helped to control the parts of our mind that relate only to the physical, in order to experience the true beauty and freedom of the higher vibrations of life.

Choosing the spiritual pathway

The first steps—when?

In common with some other people I was given the choice of my pathway in life at quite a young age. However, this can happen at any time in your life, and a spiritual awakening often occurs when there has been a crisis, such as a loved one suddenly dying, or a serious illness of your own. These events will trigger a search for answers to the meaning of life.

Some people arrive on the earth plane already committed to the spiritual pathway, and with their spiritual awareness working. There are also rare examples of wonderful spiritual leaders, some known to us all, and some who worked, and some who do work in the world without our knowledge. These are the shining lights in our world, who have decided to bless us with their physical presence, when they truly no longer belong to the earthly vibration at all.

The choice

When I was about twelve I had a vision whilst I was asleep.

I was walking along the pathway of life with everyone else and an old man, with a long beard and a branch for a walking stick, was waiting for me by the side of the road. I could see the future pathway of ordinary life, which was broad, meandering and full of people.

He then showed me the alternative spiritual pathway, which was narrow and gradually went up the mountainside, into the trees, and round a corner. I knew it went on up and up into the higher reaches of the mountain slopes.

It looked an easy pathway at the beginning, narrow but smooth, and close to the ordinary pathway of life. There was room for only one person. He told me that although it was easy at the beginning, the path got harder to travel later on, with many boulders and rough ground. There would come a point quite soon, the corner that I could see, of choice. If I continued it would be no longer possible to return to the wider pathway in the valley. There would also be further times of choice and decision later on.

But he also said that although travellers on this pathway appeared to be alone, it was not really so. He, and others, would always be with me to guide and advise and make sure that I would never fall. Sometimes I would feel that I had failed and have to backtrack, and sometimes scramble along where there seemed no pathway at all, or the path would be blocked by a huge boulder, which must be dealt with before moving onwards. But it was the road to freedom, to the light, to awe-inspiring views from the mountaintops.

I did take the spiritual pathway, otherwise I would not be writing this today.

Although it has not been an easy path, the revelations and understanding of life that I have received have meant that I have never regretted the decision.

Indeed, I know that many times in my life I would not have had the strength to carry on at all without the continual support and protection of my spiritual helpers. The clairaudient (hearing) link I have with spirit has, quite literally, saved my life several times. My willingness to give my life to spirit has, through healing, prevented me from being incapacitated through illness.

The promise that I would not be allowed to fall has been fulfilled when, without the strength and guidance of spirit, I would have left the physical life due to depression because of difficult circumstances.

I will refer back to the pathway throughout the book, so that my progress (or lack of it!) can illustrate the type of experiences involved.

However, I must stress that these examples are personal and that each journey is different. **These references will be in bold .**

How does it happen?

Once you have decided to take an interest in spiritual matters you will find that an opportunity will present itself; either you will notice an event that you can attend, or you will have a conversation with someone who will help you. When the pathway is followed, these first spiritual experiences are interesting, and taken within the security of your present life structure, at whatever point in your life this occurs.

These experiences relate to the first part of the pathway shown to me, where it is still possible to return to the wider pathway of life. When you reach the corner that takes you higher you are definitely aware of making a choice to climb higher or to go back. This is your pathway, your choices and your responsibility.

Personally, I had attended the lyceum, the Sunday school of the Spiritualist religion as a child, although I also attended conventional Sunday school with a friend. The teaching and guidance from your parents and schools form a background for your decisions as you grow older. These are not your decisions.

When I was about twelve, however, I was given the opportunity to sit in my parents' spiritual home circle, which I decided to do. This meant that I did not attend the youth club that was held that evening, although, of course, there were all the other evenings in the week for my social life. I had made room in my life for spiritual activity. My own free will was involved but this was still only a small part of my life. This first choice, however, indicated that I was interested in a spiritual course in life when offered it. This followed on from my vision of the old man.

I had set my feet on the first part of the pathway.

The first steps on the spiritual pathway after this involved visiting the Spiritualist church, again of my own free will, with my parents. I attended the healing services run by my father, and received a great deal of help for my eyesight, which was weak. Instead of my eyes weakening during puberty, as is the usual case, they were held at a reasonable level of sight, despite much studying and reading for pleasure. This was my first evidence, as a personal experience, of the power of spirit working in someone's life.

The next steps—spiritual activity

The next step is a wish to take an active rather than a passive role in the spiritual aspects of your life. You may wish to learn to heal, or you may find that the active role creeps up on you in some way. Some people find that they will begin to "know" when events are about to happen, or become more sensitive to the feelings and moods of other people. One common occurrence is that your friends, relatives and working colleagues will start to tell you their troubles, and you will try to help them.

An example of this from my own life was my first introduction to being a trance medium. When I was about sixteen my brother emigrated and my parents were concerned that they would only see him rarely for the rest of their lives. I felt a great desire to comfort them and began to feel very disturbed emotionally. I had only tried to tune in to spirit within the training circle up to this time. My father realised what was the matter and helped me to relax and calm down. The healing he gave me enabled the spirit helpers, who had drawn close, to speak through me. My parents were informed that my brother would return to Britain, but not until after my father had retired, some nine or ten years away. This did come true, but the main purpose of the message was achieved, which was to reassure them that the situation was not permanent.

This is the point where you become aware of the difference your own spiritual activity can make in other people's lives. I was so pleased to see the reassurance that my parents received, and now understood the purpose of the many months I had spent sitting in the training circle feeling that I was "doing nothing!" This had been possible because of the trigger of the love links between my parents and their children. The love vibration is always the correct link to use for spiritual communication; this power of harmony and compassion is the basis for the spiritual laws that govern life. It is important to understand that spiritual development is opposite to the development of physical skills, in that it is not apparent in the physical world until a process, or stage of development is completed.

This is because many adjustments and healing processes have to be carried out, to repair and attune your inner vibrations. This is in order to awaken the finer, more sensitive parts of your mind and relate them to the more earthly sections that you use each day. A link has to be forged for you and your inspirers to use, a channel through to your physical conscious mind from your consciousness at the other vibrations of life.

I knew at this point that I now had a choice, to continue with my training so that I could help other people and learn other spiritual skills, or return solely to my everyday teenage life and activities, and not pursue the development of my spiritual life.

The first corner of the spiritual pathway had been reached.

I can remember talking this over with my father (the spiritual teacher provided!) who reassured me that the spiritual side of my life would blend with the physical. He also said that the responsibilities of my physical life must always be attended to each day. The spiritual vibration would always be available for students of the spiritual life when earthly duties were done. Even when the physical life seemed to have taken over completely the spiritual would still be operating in the background. The experiences of life at these times would be necessary, and would be used to further my spiritual development.

I thought about my father and mother, who always both worked so hard physically, but always found time to follow their spiritual activities, of which there were many. I was impressed by the energy they possessed, even though they were so busy, and their kindness to others.

I realised I was being shown a living example of the spiritual life, and that there were many benefits, of continued health, and of personal fulfilment. Most importantly, the benefits of a release from the fear of death, and the fear of the separation from loved ones that death could bring.

So, of course, I decided to turn the corner and, though I often seemed to be doing little to further my spiritual awareness and gifts, the opportunities arose when least expected. At times in your life the opportunities do arise to develop and begin to practise your spiritual gifts, ready for when you have more room in your physical life to devote to them.

There are different ways in which you may wish to practise your spiritual gifts. You may be drawn to becoming a medium in front of the public, using your senses at the spiritual level in this way. You may find you are clairvoyant (sight), clairaudient (hearing) or clairsentient (feeling) or a combination of these faculties. Many mediums find that this communication comes into their awareness at the mental level. Their spiritual helpers or guides will use pictures or spoken words, or both, to get the message through, especially in the beginning. This use of signs and symbols is an example of the many ways in which symbols are used in spiritual development. Chapter 3 deals with this subject further. There are training circles available through most Spiritualist churches if you wish to take this option.

You may wish to take up healing, and, once again, there are many healing organisations that can help you. (There is a chapter on healing in "Wish You Were Here?") There are the gifts of physic art (inspired drawings of people in spirit or spiritual places), and of "automatic writing" (messages which are written without the medium controlling the pen.) Some mediums are able to develop trance mediumship, or channelling as it is termed in the United States, where spirit people can speak directly using the medium's voice box.

However, the spiritual pathway can be followed in many ways. Some people are drawn to yoga, for example, and find their spiritual pathway by learning, and perhaps then by teaching that discipline. Some are drawn to the healing therapies and so follow their spiritual pathway in their working lives. Doctors, nurses and carers are examples of this choice. It does not even have to be obvious that you are following the spiritual pathway. Many follow the pathway by sending out healing thoughts, for example, or working quietly to help others as a matter of course throughout their lives.

And then—working with and for spirit

Whatever way you choose to follow your own development, it begins as a separate process and gradually permeates your life. You realise that you have spiritual work to do with some of your colleagues when doing your daily job. You also discover that there are spiritual reasons for you to work in a certain place, people you were "meant" to meet for your own spiritual benefit.

In short, you become a spirit working on the earth. You are permanently aware of the reality of what is happening behind the façade of human activity, gaining insight into the true feelings and thoughts of others. You are drawn to help others, by giving out healing as you go through your day for example, and trying to create a spiritual atmosphere wherever you go.

The power to do this always comes from spirit, not from your own being. If you need more power, or need to rest, you must ask and the energy will come from spirit, and the opportunity to rest will appear. Care always must be taken not to give of your own strength, however much you sympathise with others, as this results in your own depletion.

You gradually pass the stage of working for spirit some of the time, to being a spirit working for people all the time. The stage passes when you consciously only tune in to give healing, for example, or to give spiritual messages to help people from their relatives, friends and spiritual helpers in the spirit world.

You become aware that you are listening or looking for guidance from your spiritual helpers the majority of the time. This does not mean that your life is lived for you, but as you become more aware of the consequences of your thoughts, words and deeds you naturally request more assistance to get it right.

What happens over time is that the spiritual work in your life increases and your everyday work decreases, and also that your spiritual gifts and activity increase and improve. Eventually the physical work of the world more or less fades away, or sometimes disappears quickly, and the reason for your existence on the earth becomes to work for spirit. You accept fully the fact that you are a spirit with a body and, as such, have reached the place on the pathway of being "in the world, but not of the world."

This progress, and these changes, occurs over years, and the later chapters of this book go into more detail about the background knowledge acquired along the way. Mental and emotional events and development are also explained, as the pathway gradually leads you to a different outlook and understanding of the purpose of life.

Changes in you

These changes in your life will be mirrored in changes in you. Your attitude to others will begin to alter, as will your attitude to yourself. Your understanding of life becomes more perceptive, and gradually you view events and problems from a spiritual standpoint. This means that you try to see what lesson you should be learning and to see why other people behave as they do.

These changes in your mental attitude filter through to your physical life, and you will find that you wish to change your job and your social activities. This change in your vibration will mean that some people will naturally fade out of your life and new people, in tune with your changing vibration, will enter.

You will realise how much your actions affect others and rebound upon yourself. This is the first step to self-control. Then there is the realisation that what you say to others is just as powerful and the next step must be taken. "Think before you speak," as what you say will return to you also. Finally, you understand that your very thoughts are real and your thought vibrations are where you live. We all create an atmosphere around us, which people will sense, of happiness and cheerfulness, for example, or, perhaps, of depression and sadness. Ultimately we have to attempt to control what we think.

You progress along the pathway, becoming more aware of the effect you have on other people, and aware that you are personally responsible for your own behaviour. The result should not be, however, that you do less and less, for fear of making mistakes. To do nothing is a choice also: it means that many golden opportunities are lost. You cannot stand still on the pathway of life for long, whichever pathway you have chosen.

The only constant thing in life is change, and you learn to do your best and continue whatever happens. Most people return from spirit to give the message that they regret their missed opportunities more than their mistakes. We learn from our mistakes, but a missed opportunity to give love, help or comfort, or simply to progress in life, is a chance that may not come again for a while.

Time

The way that you understand time is a good example of how your view of life alters. The understanding comes that physical age has nothing to do with the spiritual age of a person. You, in fact, begin to see with the eyes of spirit rather than just with the physical eyes. The appearance of a person becomes unimportant, and also their outer personality, as this is often not a real indication of what they are really like, any more than their physical attributes.

You begin to see time as a concept, to realise that you do not have to have your mind held in the past, or worry about the future. To begin to practise forgiveness starts to release you from the bondage of past events, and concern about what is to come. You are released into the eternal now.

You place a block on your own ability to give and receive love by holding on to hurt. It is important to receive healing as you progress, because you will need to unblock your emotions as you release yourself from previous events, and the attitudes you possess that have become part of you. The old "you" has to be left be in the past along with the others involved in a particular experience. Thus you can progress onwards with a clear and open mind.

Dealing with your fears and traumas

The fears and traumas of your nature need to be healed as you travel the pathway since they act as blocks to your spiritual development. Fear is a protective reaction, and is used by people's minds to prevent future hurt similar to that of the past. We have many fears, some coming from our body's automatic systems, some given to us by society, or passed on by other people. There are also the fears that come from our own past experiences.

Everyone has these scars on their emotions; the deep experiences of the past leave scars on the finer bodies affecting the behaviour and thought patterns in this life. These will surface throughout your life, but can be dealt with as you begin to tune in to the finer, spiritual vibrations of your mind. Personally, I discovered that I had a number of fears inbuilt that became apparent. I was afraid of dogs, but only large ones, I experienced great difficulty learning to swim, as I could not bear water to cover my face. I had a fear of ants, which seemed completely irrational. Spiders and mice, whose presence disturbs so many of us, did not worry me. One of my daughters displayed a great fear of fire from being a baby, and would never take part in bonfire night in any way.

I did not identify the causes of these fears until I began to further develop my spiritual gifts in my thirties. One by one, over about ten years, I identified the experiences that had caused the defensive fear to occur. The recollections were triggered by books and television programmes, and once by a conversation about the historical practices of execution and torture. Over a period of time there was a memory of the people involved, and this gave me a partial explanation of the reasons why my life was intertwined with theirs in the present.

Regression

Some of these recollections were not pleasant and for this reason I would comment that past life regression is not an experience to be entered into lightly, and not if you do not feel truly ready to face the past. If regression is attempted it needs to be with a qualified, recommended practitioner. It is most important that you are instructed that no pain will be felt during the memory recall, and that you will not re-experience actual physical death.

Healing is a very important factor as you progress, to deal with these past fears, and indeed, any fears from your present life. Sometimes you cannot get beyond a certain point on your pathway until a hurt has been cleared from your consciousness.

Help along the way

To progress onwards you also need to understand the signs and symbols that will come into your life to point the way. Life is full of signs and symbolic information. You have to become aware of which are of importance to you and which are irrelevant. This will be easier than it sounds as you begin to notice coincidences in your life, in names, numbers and so on, for example.

These increasing messages are there to help you to make the decisions of how far and how quickly you wish to progress, and to alert you when you are going off the pathway. I have found that *déjà vu* has shown me when I am where I should be in life. However, this will not necessarily apply to other people, as we all have our own signs and symbols. This feeling of having been somewhere before can also be a memory link from the past.

Sometimes you will leave the pathway, but you can return. Your free will and the influence of other people can take you in a different direction, but detours can be corrected. A way will always appear to return to your original intentions if you ask for this to happen. Sometimes you will need to rest from spiritual activity for a while, and sometimes everyday events will take precedence, but it is to be remembered that the pathway is an eternal one! Sometimes you will have a choice, of course, between two different pathways, which both still go upwards. It would be a hard task, indeed, if this were not the case. Free will is always yours to use at whatever stage you have reached.

Chapter 3 deals with these sign and symbols: how they can help you, and how to understand and use them to assist and not hinder your progress.

Chapter 3

Signs and Symbols—to Show the Way

LIFE is full of signs and symbols, many to do with our day-to-day affairs, but there are also many to do with various religious and spiritual beliefs and practices. There is much in our earthly existence that is symbolic of the life we will have in the spiritual spheres, as the physical life is a schoolhouse of learning for the more refined and quicker vibrations of spiritual existence.

Humans have used thousands of signs and symbols over the years to try to make sense of the world, and the experiences of life. Much of our everyday life is symbolic rather than real, sometimes twice over. For example, our paper money represents an amount in gold. However, gold itself is only worth something because we have decided to use it as a means of exchange, instead of the direct exchange of goods and food.

Thus we now have the situation of gold being dug from the ground in one part of the world, transported, and buried in vaults on the other side of the world, because of the symbolic value it has been given. The use of credit cards instead of money in recent years has taken this symbolism to a third level.

So we have to decide for ourselves what is real and of worth in our lives on the earth. Language itself is a series of symbols and signs to try to convey the reality of our thoughts to one another. We are well aware of its limitations, and the problems that can be caused by the fixed ideas that become attached to certain words and phrases over time. Translation from one language to another obviously complicates the process further. Numbers also have gathered meanings and fears around them, as have the planets in our solar system, natural events, and the plants and animals that surround us.

Somehow we have to differentiate between sense and nonsense in all this information, and decide also on the validity of the signs and symbols presented to us by the various religions and beliefs.

Positive and negative

There are positive and negative symbols, and it is easy to become worried by negativity. It is important to realise that positive thought is stronger than negative, although both have their part to play in the balance of life. What we call destruction has to come into play to take away what is no longer needed so that a new start can occur. There should be a balance between active and passive, positive and negative etc. in life. Difficulties occur when over-emphasis is placed on the "breaking-down" elements with no replacement of "building up" with a new beginning. The building-up processes associated with new helpful ideas link with the creative force of life, and a channel is provided for power to come from the higher, harmonious vibrations of life.

The energy of life can be used in either way. Negative thoughts and actions, however, will link with the "breaking-down" vibrations and naturally result in the disintegration of the activity involved. Therefore symbols used in a negative way can be dealt with by a positive mirror image. This, and any other spiritual cleansing activity, should never be attempted alone and not when you are unsure of yourself. Light always overcomes darkness; even the small flame of a struck match will give light in total darkness. Light from the highest source is what to ask for and visualise when dealing with negative conditions.

Signs and symbols are tools

Most people find symbols attractive and useful, but it is important to remember that they are tools to aid understanding, and do not have to become so important that you cannot function without them. Simplicity is helpful with any symbols and signs you use, and you must always remember that all of us are directly linked to the Creator of life and can communicate our thoughts and feelings directly if we wish.

Because symbols and signs are only tools, they do not have to take over and control the spiritual life. This lesson is one being learnt at the moment by all the religions of the world. All religions in essence teach the same principles of love and the unity of all life but viewed from different angles. Each religion concentrates to some extent on a different aspect of truth, for example, the peace of Buddhism.

But each religion has the fundamental basis of the reality of one creative force of life, called by different names. Spiritual truth is all religions combined, but the symbols, signs and written testaments used by each religion can act as blocks to this unity, and fetters to the human mind.

The different interpretations of religions appeal to different people because we all look at life in our own way, and are each on our own pathway, learning at our own level and learning our particular lessons. Therefore a particular religion will be suitable for one person and not another. Following the spiritual pathway means that we should try to be tolerant of each other's beliefs and to see the other person's point of view. The whole of our reality cannot be expressed whilst living in the material world, and therefore we find it difficult to accept the wholeness of religious thought when our minds are linked to the physical expression of life.

However, each soul will reach a point where their mind combines and rises above particular interpretations and the related symbols, and begins to comprehend that there is truly only one creative force, one created universe and one family of created life. This universe stretches from the material vibration through to the finer vibrations of harmonious love that we can only begin to imagine.

Natural signs and symbols

The signs and symbols in the natural world are often the most useful and easy to understand. There are familiar old sayings such as "a red sky at night," that acts as a helpful shorthand to reading the weather for the next day, for example. These are based on observations and fact. We are part of the natural world and its contents are there to provide us with physical life. We often use parts of nature as symbols, the "tree of life" being one of the most used to explain various ideas.

These are often the most useful because nature is the link from this world to the next. The spiritual guidance we receive on our journey will use natural symbols to take us on our spiritual pathway away from the physical to a spiritual existence.

Signs and symbols in mediumship and meditation

In mediumship

Mediums are continually passing messages on to people and trying to make clear what their loved ones and helpers wish to communicate to the receiver. To make this communication quicker, clearer and easier mediums are often given symbols from spirit, often individual to each medium, although some symbols are used which are generally accepted. This speeds up the process and avoids misunderstandings. It can also be helpful when dealing with information of a personal nature, which the medium can then represent easily without knowing any details.

Personally I have found that my collection of symbols has grown over the years I have been working, but have also found that symbols are not used at all when they are not needed. My spirit inspirers will use symbols or familiar phrases to give me information about events for my own information, or to quickly let me know how I am progressing. One example of this is that I discovered that I would start to sing a particular song for no reason, just before a famous person associated with that song was about to depart the physical life.

Often someone wishing to communicate will use an object or picture that has immediate meaning to the receiver but seems strange to the medium. If you wish to work as a spiritual messenger this information has to be allowed to flow through your mind and be given out no matter how odd it sounds. This is one of the most difficult techniques to master, as nervousness makes you question what you are receiving, and we are not used to speaking in public thoughts which are not our own.

In meditation—symbolic pictures

In meditation, symbols are used to make a link for us from the physical to the spiritual worlds. Meditation and visualisation techniques use symbols, pictures in the mind, drawing on the imagination to link the physical level of thought to the etheric and astral levels of life.

The mind has levels of thought, some of which link totally to the physical life, but there are many that function apart from the physical. Imagination and dreams, daydreams and theoretical plans have a separate existence to our physical actions. Meditation blends these different levels of thought to create a reality for you to cross to the spiritual world. Meditation is a tool provided for you to create a thought bridge in your mind. We are always creators whether we like it or not!

Nature is the natural link between the spheres of life. One of the easiest meditations is one that uses a pleasant familiar place of restfulness, your favourite place, for you to begin to create a link for yourself. (There is more on how this link develops in "Wish You Were Here?" in the meditation chapter.)

Colours and numbers are symbols to explain the concepts of spiritual life to the mind whilst held in the physical experience. The importance of colours is explained in this chapter. The use of numbers, to give us an idea of the other levels of life apart from the physical, is given in "Wish You Were Here?" in the chapter "The Spheres of Life Beyond the Physical World."

These symbolic pictures link through to become reality, as we truly live in our spirit using our mind to link where we wish to link. When we dream, for example, that is our reality. It is possible to gain control of our dream state, to know we are dreaming, and this is another way we can find a link to the other spheres of life. An example of this linking is the symbol of a waterfall. Water symbolises emotion, the water of life, and water is seen as a cleanser of emotions, just as it cleanses our physical bodies. The river of life has to be crossed to reach the spiritual levels, a concept that has been accepted in human thought for many years. Where you cross this river determines where you arrive on the other side. To cross over at the top of the waterfall you have to climb the pathway on this side of the river all the way up. You cannot go behind the waterfall to blend with your higher self at that level unless you have expressed true love, unconditional love, for someone else in your life.

Thus the symbol has acted as a release for the mind from the physical life and has become the reality for you to experience. Where meditation has been practised, or even if these realities are only accepted, the transition from this world to the next, via this or another route, is greatly eased.

Colours—their spiritual symbolic importance

The colours of the natural world and the way we see them have much importance for us. We understand the healing influence of golden sunshine, and the soothing, calming influence of green trees and plants. This colour coding is to help us to be healthy in mind, body and spirit, to keep the balance of our being in our busy lives.

Chakras

There are energy centres in every person, often called chakras (Sanskrit for wheel), as the study of these centres is involved in the theory and practice of yoga. I first learnt this information when

I began to study yoga in the 1980s, and since then it has become more widely known.

The aim is to understand the linking of the spirit through the mind and emotions to the body, using these energy centres. These centres are commonly associated with different colours, and there are seven. You link to the physical through these, and they are to do with the emotional and spiritual parts of your nature rather than the physical body. There are indications of this in our descriptions of feeling emotions, for example, our gut instinct, the heart bursting with happiness and the experience of heartache, the head being too full of thought and so on.

Briefly, the chakras are as follows:

Base chakra—located around the base of the spine and associated with red.
Sacral chakra—the groin area and orange.
Solar plexus chakra—the navel area and yellow.
Heart chakra—the centre of the chest and green.
Throat chakra—associated with blue.
Brow chakra—the " third eye" (spiritual vision) and indigo.
Crown chakra—the top and centre of the head and purple.

The healing we all receive from the green expanses of nature is most important because green is the colour linked with the heart chakra, giving emotional balance. This is a blending of the yellow of the solar plexus, associated with instinctive feelings and worldly intelligence, and the blue of the throat for speech and the communication of our thoughts. The personal feelings centred on the heart chakra are a blend of the yellow and blue, a bridge between the lower and higher functions of the person. This is where the reactions relating to the physical blend with the speech and thought, resulting in personal emotional reactions. The green of nature is positioned similarly between the red, orange and yellow fire of the physical inner world and the blue of the sky.

Food

As my link with my spirit helpers improved, they explained to me that the edible plants, fruit and meat are colour coded for us to recognise what we need to eat. We need to consume green vegetables, for example, to restore or retain our physical and emotional balance. Our bodies will tell us what we need if we will notice what food appeals to us each day and not fall into a rigid pattern or listen only to the opinion of other people.

Some days, for example, we fancy tomatoes, lettuce and an apple, but bananas have no appeal. Of course a balance has to be struck to be healthy, but that balance can be achieved using the food which is in tune with our needs that day.

It is not only food which is colour coded for us, although this is an interesting introduction. In fact the entire physical world is linked to our perception of colour, to represent to us our growth and progress from the physical concept of life to the reality of a spiritual existence.

How colours portray spiritual progress

The colours of chakras represent the progress of your spiritual growth through various stages. The colour red is strongly linked with the physical life, orange with children and earthly creation, yellow with worldly work and intellect, green with emotional life, blue with verbal expression, indigo with seeing life properly, and purple with thought, that does not necessarily link to the physical world at all.

The colours gradually take the consciousness away from expression centred on physical activity, through to a realisation of the importance of feelings. From here the person travels on to the expression of thoughts and the important links between thought, feeling, and activity. Then comes the final realisation that it is possible to live in the mind, and that the chain is from mind to thought to feelings to action.

Your reality in the physical comes through from your spirit via this chain, represented by the colours. The higher your aspiration the closer to your original creative intention your actions become. Obviously it is very easy for us all to be influenced along the way, and this is the way we learn. Free will gives us the choice to choose the influences we follow. When we follow the highest and best in a moral sense, then we progress and our colour vibrations become clearer and brighter.

The colours give an aid to progress, so that you can use them as a way of understanding and improving your reality. The aura that some sensitive people can see is the colours of your vibration, which are always changing and moving as your thoughts and feelings alter. The more control you gain of your own nature, the more harmonious your reality becomes. This means that spiritual energy can easily flow from your spirit through your more refined bodies, then through the astral body, and finally to the etheric body and through to the physical form.

Life takes us on a natural progression through the colours, beginning with physical activity and organising our physical life. We make a relationship with another person. Then we move on to relationships with children, often our own, or other creative work at a physical level. Then we learn to use worldly intelligence to organise our lives and balance these demands on our time.

This all brings much emotional content into our lives and this organisation has to take into account our emotional reactions. We have to understand that emotions and reason are equally important. Eventually we have to let our children lead their own lives, for example, and go through the experience of losing loved ones to their further progression in spirit.

We have to realise that we also will leave the earth one day and these experiences happen to everyone. We have to try to give unconditional love, which is the expression of true love, and thus blend the red of our physical nature with the blue, and reach a spiritual understanding of life and the purple vibration.

All this is not accomplished easily, of course, and we have the continual assistance of our individual conscience to let us know how well we are doing!

The capability to express yourself properly at each colour vibration has to be learned, from the control and proper use of the physical action of the body, the control and proper expression of the emotions, through to the control and positive use of thought. These capabilities have to be combined into a harmonised and balanced whole. Healing is important at this stage because each facet of your nature has to be cleared and correctly aligned before this combination can be successful. A complete, harmonious, individualised person has been formed ready to exist at a spiritually centred level of existence.

The chakra colours will alter as you progress and learn to develop your spiritual nature. The relationship that you have with your physical body changes because of your growing awareness of the other vibrations or bodies of your existence. Therefore the colour and vibration of your energy centres reflect the difference, the range of vibration you use will increase, and the link to the spiritual vibrations of life will open up more and more. At what stage these alterations begin to happen is discussed in Chapter 4, but the first signs of progress are usually linked with the opening and development of the third eye chakra. The awareness of spiritual vibrations through the senses in some way begins to occur, not necessarily as vision, as each person is different.

There are also fourth, fifth, and sixth centres progressing up the centre of the forehead, which will open as spiritual awareness increases. When the crown chakra is reached it will open at the white vibration, which includes all colours, and a channel will be made for the golden beam of the life force to travel through the centre of the crown chakra down through all the chakra centres of the body.

The physical life—a schoolhouse of learning

One of the most useful symbolic representations used by spirit to explain why we are in the physical life, with all its trials and tribulations, is this concept of a schoolhouse. It embodies several truths about our lives: the fact that our experiences are lessons, that we should be trying to progress from class to class, and that our whole lives are but a preparation for the real life of the spiritual world after the death of the physical body.

This progression of the spirit through the experiences of physical lives is a continuing process. I am sure that we are all aware that the earth is populated by people who are at many differing stages of this long process, and some who do not seem to have even begun! However, it is part of our learning process to understand this and try to be tolerant of other people's behaviour. There will be those who are ahead of us, of course, and we will be grateful for their tolerance of our behaviour.

There are indications to demonstrate our position to us in this schoolhouse. We are aware when we have gone up a class as life suddenly becomes more difficult, and we are faced with people, situations and choices that we are not sure how to handle. Demands are made of us that were not there before. I mistakenly believed that I was an unselfish, patient person until I had children of my own and discovered that my life had, in fact, been quite self-centred up to that point.

Often we get the same lesson over again until we have learned to deal with the experience. "Why does this keep happening to me?" we cry. When it stops happening it is because we have changed our attitude in some way, and have altered our vibration, therefore, to bring ourselves another aspect of life.

We know we are ready to move on because we become bored with our lives and say things like, "I wish something would happen!" This is when care has to be taken that we do not make something happen that we later regret. So it can perhaps be observed that we are never satisfied, but I think that this is part of the continual striving of the spirit filtering through from our true reality.

This concept of a schoolhouse of learning applies to everyone, and applies to all the pathways of life. It is linked with the idea of the spiritual pathway, however, in the following way.

The schoolhouse links to the pathway

Eventually you reach the point when you begin to learn to be a teacher! Of course it must always be remembered that you still continue to learn, often from your pupils, which is a necessarily humbling experience. This wish to help others and pass on what you have learned in life, rather than just concentrate on your own experiences, is an indication that you are wishing to tread the spiritual pathway.

When you begin this process it is a part of your life only and then gradually permeates how you react to other people and how you treat them. To try to heal and assist becomes a way of life, and, no matter how many difficulties and rebuffs you encounter, it is not possible to return to your former behaviour. The main lesson that has be learned here is that everyone must be allowed to express their free will and you can only offer help and advice. Often this is rejected, which is an upsetting process, but people cannot be forced to do what you consider is correct for them. There is the possibility, of course, that you could be wrong!

The only true way to teach anything is by good example, and it is also the most difficult method of all. It is an observable fact that if you have children, they will take the way you behave, and the way you live your life, as your teaching. "Do as I say, not as I do," is not successful!

The pathway—symbols become reality

This spiritual progress continues, enabling the spirit to travel along the spiritual pathway into spirit, away from the physical life altogether, and then up and up into the other spheres of spiritual life. The correct use of symbols and signs in a spiritual way, lead us to the understanding that the physical world in which we live is itself a symbol, a restricted and incomplete reality.

The spiritual pathway itself is, of course, a symbol also, to help us to understand where we have reached in our life's progress, creating a mental reality for us to use to reach the next levels of life. Thus we can see the proper use of a symbol demonstrated for us by our spiritual inspirers, who use this representation of a pathway to free us from our limited existence, and not to restrict or restrain our ideas.

We have to practise our creativity at the slowest and most cumbersome of vibrations, the physical. Then we can progress to quicker vibrations of more dimensions, with bodies that are more receptive, more powerful and refined, that can express more and more of the reality of our true spiritual being and intent. These bodies, in turn, have to be grown out of and comprehended to be a restriction of the expression of the soul. These lower selves have to be released, as the physical body is released, as the soul progresses. The lesson is that we have to give up our lower self each time in order to progress, in order to become a larger, more refined version of our own being.

We find this very difficult at first, but there is no choice about giving up the physical body: there comes a time when we are released from it by natural law, if by no other way. The releasing of the self at other levels of life is less traumatic because the permanent reality of life has been accepted, as has the truth that the link between those that love one another can never be broken. Thus, we progress to this realisation that the physical world is only a representation of the worlds at the finer vibrations of life. The whole of the physical universe is a symbolic creation of the higher realities of existence; the physical is the outer coating of the universe, symbolic of the worlds waiting for us to experience— a "virtual," temporary and restricted reality.

So we have been led away from one reality of physical existence by what we thought of as symbols, which have gradually formed into the reality of the next phase of our existence at a more refined vibration of life. Life is opposite to what we think it is whilst encased in the physical body. Our time linked to the physical is such a restriction of our reality it is, in fact, the closest we will come to what we term death. When we are released into the spiritual life we will realise then, if not before, that our lives of health, happiness and creative fulfilment have just begun. What we term death is the beginning of our true life.

The physical life—marks in the sand

Our physical lives have been explained to me like scratching a mark with a stick in the sands of time. First of all we manage to scratch a small line, to make our mark on life, however small it might be. We learn to make a longer and longer line, and then comes the difficult task of turning a corner. This is when we face a traumatic time in our life and have to do battle with large problems. It can take several attempts before we do not let this defeat us but find the courage to carry on with our life. It is the work of a lifetime to make a small scratch in the sand, but each time we progress further.

It appears at this point that we have achieved a great deal and now understand much more about ourselves and other people. We can continue to go forward and continue our line in a new direction. However, we cannot continue in the same pattern forever and eventually another corner has to be turned. Different problems are faced, new difficulties and changes, consequences of past actions and hurtful truths. Once more it can take more than one attempt to turn this corner, and begin anew as a more progressed version of yourself, in another direction again.

There is the opportunity to release on the straight parts of the pathway, depending on where we have reached before. We have then to return to tackle the next corner next time. We are not supposed to give up at the corners, but, of course, often do. This is when we have to remember that life is eternal and another chance will come eventually.

Surely, we think, when we reach the third straight course, this struggle must be over now. But we are learning to draw a square, the square of physical life, because four is the number for physical expression. (This square of physical life is referred to in "Wish You Were Here?" in The Spheres of Life Beyond the Physical World, Sphere 9.) So, there is another corner to be turned to reach the last straight, with new lessons and hurtful experiences, and again it is extremely hard not to give up the fight.

Turning these corners is an illustration of our progress as a person, and we gain in that invaluable asset, personal experience, with each successful new beginning. When the third corner has been turned we are on the home run as we are heading back towards the point at which we came in to the physical vibration. The possession or non-possession of a physical body then becomes immaterial (a joke from my inspirers!), as the person is then living and experiencing life at the spiritual vibration.

The body indeed becomes like a coat which is put on and taken off, but does not interfere with the awareness of spiritual reality. You begin to experience spiritually yourself, rather than just being aware of the contact to you from your inspirers. Gradually, a life at different levels begins, in meditation or dream state or impinging on the physical when conscious.

The last corner completes the square and we have released ourselves from the physical expression of life necessary for our own development. We can continue our journey on the next vibration of life. It has probably been noticed as you have read this chapter that each of these symbolic representations has brought the person involved to the same place, the end of necessary individual development in the physical world and the beginning of the spiritual life.

There is a spiral of gold in the centre of the square, which is the golden cord of the life force present everywhere, holding all life together in one whole. The next progression is to the concept of a triangle, which occurs on a spiritual vibration. After this we travel in a circle, which is the basis for the spiral of life.

Some ways of telling how far you have progressed on your pathway and what it means to accept each new stage are covered in Chapter 4.

The progression to the concept of a triangle and then the circle of life are explained in Chapters 5 and 6.

Chapter 4

Where Am I on the Pathway – How Far Have I Got?

THE concept of the pathway is a symbol in itself, as stated in the last chapter, because we are at the stage of our development when we need obvious assistance to find our way, something that our understanding of life in the three dimensional world can incorporate and use. You will generally realise how far you have travelled along the pathway by how you relate to other people and the way they live. The more you engage in spiritual work, the more your attitude to life, and therefore your interests, alters.

Chapter 2 explained the changes you will notice in your life and yourself as you start to follow the pathway. You will be able to see for yourself how much you have altered when you meet people from your past who have not changed. The amount of spiritual activity in your life and to what extent you have revised your thinking on life gives an indication of your progress.

Important principles

Comparison

One of the first, most important, principles to grasp is that there is no need to be concerned where you are on this pathway compared to other people. Each person treads their own pathway, and there are always people ahead of you to give help, and those who have not reached your understanding whom you can help. Even so, this is only a general observation, and you will often find that someone will possess a better understanding of life in one respect and you in another. In this way we learn to help one another on an equal basis with sympathy and without judgement.

Loneliness

We also have to grasp that we are never alone on our journey, especially when we are struggling the most. We all find it difficult to ask for help when we most need it, as we think of it as an admission of failure. In fact we need to request help when we are in the greatest need of it so that we will not fail!

There is an increasing alteration in the relationship you have with the ordinary, everyday world, and a deep sense of loneliness at times. However, as you discover friends who are interested in your new way of looking at life, and become accustomed to behaving differently yourself, this loneliness retreats. You will develop an increasing awareness of, and communication with your own spiritual helpers, and learn to accept their help as a normal part of life.

Slow and steady wins the race

It is most important to understand that your "mental feet" should be kept firmly on the ground of common sense, and each step in knowledge should pass the test of your logical mind. You are building your own nature and future and, just as with physical buildings, the foundations must be deep and solid before you begin to climb. We are used to being concerned about time in our daily lives, but with spiritual progression you are embarking on an eternal process, and time is unimportant. Many of the assumptions we accept in our material lives are reversed for spiritual life; for example, we are often progressing the most spiritually when nothing seems to be going well for us. It is then we learn patience and strength of purpose, and experience the suffering that will give us our compassion for others in the future. Our achievements made in this way will change our character, and will be permanent, our progress changing the reality of our true nature forever.

Adjustment between spiritual and earthly vibrations

One of the major differences we will find when we leave the physical to live in the dimensions of life away from the earth is the co-operative nature of the life and activity. Teamwork is the normal procedure there, with equal appreciation and value given to each member. Effort is harmoniously combined, and help is automatically given one to another for the achievement of a particular aim.

As we begin to link with our spiritual helpers and experience their understanding and compassion, it can be difficult to adjust to the difference between their vibration and the working vibrations of the world. It is at this stage that you can feel the need to change your work, or adopt a different attitude to the work you are involved in, to cope with the variation in the vibrations of life you are experiencing. The changes in your own mental and emotional nature need to be reflected in your environment.

Levels of your mind

Another aspect of this same adjustment between the two differing vibrations is an opposing feeling from the everyday mind when spiritual activity is considered. The function of this "physical" part of the mind is to keep body and soul together and therefore the development of increased spiritual awareness triggers the alert mechanism. The "body mind," as my father used to term it, has to be controlled, reassured and understood. It is a question of mind over matter, and is part of the process of tuning in to another vibration of existence.

How to find out—ask to be shown

We only have to ask for an indication of our progress if we wish to understand where we are, or what our choices are for the next step. This information will reach us in different ways. If you do not have astral experiences or find meditation difficult, as this depends very much on the person, the information will come into your everyday life. It can come as a symbol, a picture or song, or perhaps something will be said to you that answers your question, although the other person will probably not realise this is happening.

If you are used to using symbols or receiving messages from mediums it can easily be shown to you this way. What we experience in our sleep state is often the method used to show us our progress, but care must be taken here. Many dreams are linked to the physical and coloured by the present emotional state, and physical condition, of the person involved. Often, the true reality of what is experienced in the other dimensions of life is lost and distorted on the return journey to physical consciousness.

If you need to do preparation or training you will find the opportunity will come, and also you will know when it is time to leave a certain situation. When it is time to begin some spiritual work, again the opportunity will be given to you, and then, of course, you can use your free will to take this chance or not.

How will I know if it is time to begin spiritual work?

You only have to send up the thought that you wish to know if it is time for you to begin, or whether you need to have more experiences or learn more spiritual theory. The answer will come to you in one of the ways explained.

I described in Chapter 2 how I knew when I had reached the first corner of the pathway and would not be returning to the wider pathway in the valley of life. After this I was very busy with the earthly experiences of education, career, marriage and children. The only major spiritual happenings in my teenage years were firstly my realisation that I could ask to be released from a particular dream where I appeared to have got "stuck!" (This is recounted in Chapter 2 of "Wish You Were Here?"), and then the message that was given to my parents about my brother, as mentioned earlier in this book.

When my children had passed the baby stage I did ask the question of whether it was time for my spiritual work to begin, when out for a family walk. I was immediately directed to a church we were approaching. When we entered the church I was instructed to read the page open in the church bible. It was the passage that informs us that all spiritual gifts are worthless unless we have love for our fellow humans. I knew that I was to concentrate on giving love and compassion, and that any gifts that I should develop must be used to serve and help other people or I would be wasting my time.

Soon after this I was given the chance to study yoga and began to give healing to a friend who had an incurable eye condition that had made her virtually blind. It took some courage to offer her healing as I was not sure what her reaction would be, but she accepted. I was so pleased when her sight recovered enough for her to cross the road safely and to be able to read large print books.

The spiritual work of my adult life had begun. It was time to continue the pathway.

Indications of where you are—different representations along the way

We can be shown representations of the pathway and our spiritual progress along it in different ways. Our physical life, spiritually speaking, can be shown by the pathway as it goes up the mountain of physical life, as given at the beginning of the book. This will link to physical circumstances and people and show the spiritual reality of the events and relationships in our lives. When the top of the mountain is reached the person is released into the spiritual life. That particular mountain has been climbed, and progress can be continued in spirit, at least for the time being. There may well be a need to return for more physical experiences later.

Our personal mental, emotional and spiritual progress along the pathway can be shown to us in many ways, which involve stiles into fields, stepping stones over streams, and bridges. Buildings or places can be seen as a background, either ones from our lives—a school perhaps—or sometimes places from another level of our existence.

Physical places

Physical places do have a spiritual counterpart, their spiritual reality that can be visited. You can visit these places when you are asleep and people can come from spirit to see you. We are all creating a reality for ourselves as we live our lives. This is often the easiest way of meeting your loved ones, in the spiritual counterpart of their home, a favourite garden, or building.

When my father died I attended a service for his ascension when I was asleep, in the spiritual equivalent of the church in which he worked the most, and where his physical funeral service was conducted. Around the walls were representations of all the work of his life, and there were many people there, attending his spiritual celebration of his life and his passing to the next stage. Some of them still had physical bodies, and some were present who had passed onwards to the spirit life, and returned for this meeting. I walked with him from the church after the service until we reached a bridge, which I crossed with him to halfway. Then he had to progress onwards and I had to stop, as it was not my time to enter the spiritual side of life.

Interlinking

These different representations of the pathway do interlink, and other people will often be involved. The more spiritual visions, which are less related to actual backgrounds from your daily life, will show the reality of your relationships with other people rather than physical circumstances. This assists you when difficult decisions have to be made, or you have to adjust to trying circumstances.

As these pictures become more linked to spiritual reality, you will see the people you are linked with more clearly, either by their behaviour in your experience, or by an alteration in their age. Someone who is quite old physically can appear as a child, for example, if your helpers wish to indicate that, spiritually speaking, the person is still young.

Sometimes you will be an observer of others, to help you to understand a situation in your life, or in the world generally. Often you will be shown your own behaviour in relation to others, or given a choice when in meditation or in the physical sleep state on the astral planes. Your natural choice will show you the true state of your mind on certain matters.

However, you can always send a thought from your conscious mind afterwards to your helpers on how you wish to progress and alter, or that you would like to make amends. All these states of your mind are linked and you will be given the opportunity to improve matters. This, of course, is the whole object of the exercise!

In meditation & sleep state

We wish, of course, not to be separated from our loved ones by the physical barrier of time and the losing of the physical body. Meditation is most useful here, as the consciousness is released under prepared conditions. This is especially true where the meditation is guided by a spiritual instructor, who can help you to visualise a place where your own inspirers can meet you. The experiences can, therefore, be more reliable than what is retained by the mind after physical sleep. The chapter on meditation in "Wish You Were Here?" gives examples of how these different stages can be represented for you, to travel away from your mind's physical reality to the reality of other levels of life.

However, the states of meditation and what we experience in sleep state can be linked and combined. The dream state can be controlled and understood, if you wish to undertake the mental training necessary for this process. Dreams about physical life and dream experiences just beyond the physical can be left behind. One of the first steps is to realise that you are dreaming, as your will is then beginning to take control of your experience. This dream controlling and escaping to another level is something you have to ask for and then the assistance will arrive.

If we do not recognise places from our physical life it is because a meditation is linking into the other dimensions of life away from the physical. There are doors and stairways, and some people experience going down a corridor with many doors to open. Sometimes there are roads to cross. These all lead us into an awareness of the etheric and astral realities available to us at our present stage of development.

Sleep state

It is important to understand that when we talk about "dreams," "sleep state," and "astral projection," we are talking about differing vibrations for the spirit to experience, using the mind to understand and record them.

It is only the body that sleeps, and our mind remains active, whether we remember in the morning or not. We generally use the term "dreams" to cover mind pictures from our daily lives through to experiences relating to other realities in spirit life. Therefore I have used the term "sleep state" instead of "dream state" to cover all these experiences, as many of our experiences whilst our bodies sleep are as real as or more real than physical ones.

Passing over

When people experience physical death the helpers who guide them can often, though not always, use transport of some kind to take them from the physical, a train, a ship, or a coach. This needs to be transport that is not controlled by the person so that they will accept the experience and not try to return until they have recovered from the initial shock of discovering that they have passed over and their physical body is no longer available. These modes of transport can also be used in meditation and the sleep state to visit people you wish to see on the other side of life.

Visiting loved ones in spirit

We are able to visit loved ones at a halfway house where there are reception rooms where souls can be together when some are in physical and some in spirit. These meetings are the usual procedure, although, of course, some of us remember them well and some do not.

In order to visit loved ones further away from the physical vibration than the halfway houses, we have to conquer our natural fear of the loss of the physical body, or death as it is known. We have to face complete darkness, and also not be afraid to visit them consciously through any colour vibration.

I had to remember a previous experience where the fear of death conquered me. I had lost someone very close to me and despaired. This time I remembered my previous mistake and was conscious of walking with the loved one each side of a dividing impenetrable fence and accepting the situation this time, knowing that it was temporary. After braving this complete dark linked to despair I found myself, in my next experience, talking to a lady I had helped who explained that I had earned a visit beyond the bridge between physical and next level of life. Love and kindness is always the key.

We experience this darkness when we are born into the physical and again when we are born into the next phase of life. It is just a temporary passage as we go from one vibration to another.

Waterfalls, bridges, doors and stairs—to show your progress clearly

These representations along the pathway of stiles, bridges, stairs and doors are to help us adjust as we ascend to tune in with the different understanding and appearance of life at the different spiritual vibrations. We are all familiar with the concept of a bridge from this world to the next, which is one way in which the mountain pathway links up with the pathway as it ascends to the next vibrations of life. This is used as I have just described in my personal experience of my father's progression.

There are many ways to link through from the physical state of mind to the realms of spiritual life. Over the years my helpers and instructors in spirit have shown me various alternatives.

Waterfalls and beyond

For example I have found myself in meditation and in astral travel at a waterfall as described in the chapter on symbols. The pathway of life led away from the physical, through a garden and out into nature, coming out at the side of the waterfall, where it was a steep climb to the top. I knew that I had come away from the physical life and was going to link with a more spiritual version of my own reality. The only way to reach the waterfall and pass behind it to find your next self at this level, is by reaching the vibration of true love, unconditional love for another person. It is possible to cross the river at lower points and find other expressions of your spiritual reality.

The pathway then continues on the other side of the river, leading to a small temple where you are helped to ascend to the next level of life. You are escorted along the pathway and encouraged to enter the temple, the door of which you must open yourself. This is the entrance to spirit life, the meeting place for your lower and higher selves. There is a circle of white light in the centre of the circular room inside the temple, and there are progressed spiritual helpers sitting around the edge of the room. You are helped to stand on the circle and not be afraid. You have a sensation of rising and find yourself in an entrance hallway at another level of life. You can then be shown many different places and people at various vibrations of spiritual life, depending upon your progression, understanding and wishes.

I had a time in my life when I spent several weeks astral travelling and meditating in this way, which produced the information about the spheres of life beyond the earth as described in my first book. The most difficult part of these experiences was when I was informed that I had to return my main consciousness to the physical plane of life as I still had much to do.

Doors of colour

One of the most helpful examples of gateways to the next levels of life that I have been shown is a series of doors of different colours, relating to the chakras as described earlier. A Chinese gentleman, who titles himself "Sunshine" for working from spirit with us on the earth, as he is so cheering, has been helping me for many years with trance work, inspirational addresses, and messages from people in spirit. He worked with my father before myself and often describes his beautiful garden full of orange trees and peaceful walks, where he cares for our family pets who have passed over to spirit.

In a meditation he showed me this series of doors at the end of an avenue of trees in his garden. He explained that people could visit him when asleep, and he would help them to go through the doors into the vibration of life linked with each particular colour. Each coloured door is progressively harder to open, the red being the easiest as it is the colour relating to the physical vibration of life.

We can travel to and fro through the red door using our etheric body, which links closely with the physical, as we learn to control the basics of material existence. We all use all the different colours in our lives, of course, making the rainbow of our lives.

These doors, however, link to spheres of spiritual life and are one way to travel over the rainbow of physical expression into spiritual activity, and the use and understanding of colours as spiritual tools. The other doors require the use of the astral body, which can act independently from the physical understanding. This brings experiences to the mind that are not connected to the daily life. We all have experiences when we are asleep in the spiritual spheres that we can reach. Learning to use these doors, however, means that you can have some memory of your activities brought back to your physical consciousness.

One of the most difficult to open is the green door as it links to the emotional nature and the proper expression of emotions towards other people. The correct balance and blending of the yellow and blue to produce a beautiful green takes most of us a long time to achieve. There can be no pretence, of course; if you have not yet achieved proper compassionate understanding and expression of emotion the door will not open.

The purple door is the last one and the hardest of all. The red energy of the physical has to be combined correctly with the blue of expressed thought in speech. The power of these two main aspects of your being, physical action and mental action, has to be controlled, balanced with each other, and expressed on a vibration of unconditional love and compassion. As you pass through this door you step into an almost blinding light, as the colours make up the white vibration, in the same way as the colours of the rainbow are contained in physical light. You have gained access to the white vibrational sphere of spiritual life, by the understanding and proper use of the colours from red through to purple.

There will be indications in your life to show which colour or colours you are dealing with, and with which colour or colours other people are currently involved. Quite apart from these colours that act as an indication of your present state, each person has their own colour or colours of vibration that are individual to them. These act as a spiritual fingerprint, the natural vibration of that person expressed in colour, and each person's colour or colours are different.

You will find that you harmonise easily with people who are complementary colours to yourself, and less easily with others, also depending on the spiritual age of the person involved.

However, you will be able to tell what colour vibration you are dealing with at the moment by the important emphasis in your life, yellow for mental study for example. The people you meet will give you experiences that improve your understanding and control of this aspect of life, and many of them will have the natural spiritual colour vibration that you are linking with at that time.

So these colours take the pathway through the vibration energy levels and are portals into spirit. Each coloured door links through to another sphere of life until you are able to link to the white sphere. The understanding of colour has been taken to a higher mental interpretation and you are learning to use the colours as these spiritual tools for your own progression. The emphasis of your thinking has been gradually drawn away from a physical centring to a spiritual reality to show you the progress of your soul.

This means that you are looking at life in a new way, from a viewpoint of eternal progress and you begin to realise that service to others is the key to a successful spiritual life. You will discover that you will be served as you serve others. A life lived with understanding and compassion for the problems of other people is more fulfilling than one with the purpose of personal material gain.

Stairs to climb, step by step

Stairs are a very clear indication of exactly how far you have progressed and my helpers linked this to the different colours to make it even clearer. In this way the pathway leads further away from the physical vibration into the spiritual reality of your life and development. It is important to remember that although spiritual progress often seems painstakingly slow, and lessons have to be repeated, once something has been truly learned, that progress is yours forever.

I was shown the pathway from the yellow to green to blue vibrations by a stairway. I found myself in a large hallway, where there were many people, which I knew I had entered from the physical vibration of life. My spiritual helpers were with me but stood slightly behind me so that I could not really see them. This is a usual experience as they wish you to concentrate on what they are showing you.

Green stairs

In front of me were some green stairs that I knew I had been asking to climb. I was handed a round disc with a symbol in black, which indicated that it had been misused on earth. They explained that I had to turn it over and fill in the symbol with white light with my mind to purify it and counteract the other side. I knew that this would act as a future balance to prevent this symbol being used wrongly again. Then I was able to climb the green stairs. When I reached the top there was a landing and a green door into what I knew was the spiritual vibration of life at that level. I was aware that I now had the choice to go through the door or continue with the next set of stairs that were to be blue.

This was when I realised that this had been the second time I had climbed the green stairs as each person has to "lay the carpet" of colour on their stairs. As a result of mistakes I had made I had had to return to the beginning of the green and climb again. This, in fact, explained to me why some people were involved in unpleasant experiences of mine in my present life and previous lives, as their lack of progress was due to this mistake of mine at an earlier stage. Thus it was brought home to me how important forgiveness of oneself and others is and how intertwined we all are.

This also illustrates the principle mentioned earlier about spiritual progress needing to be taken slowly and one step at a time, because you are building your own future and state of being. If you rush and make mistakes you will have to do that part again! It also illustrates that the green vibration is indeed one of the really difficult progressions to master. You are learning to harmonise and combine two parts of your own nature to deal with other people on a proper love vibration. A battle with the ego is involved, and you are experiencing the first attempt at truly showing love to others even if they are unlike you or even actively in opposition to yourself.

It is plain to see how difficult this is, and, although we may wish to behave in this way, theory is very different to practice. All religious beliefs and people are worthy of equal consideration, and prejudice has to be put to one side.

I did link through to spirit through the green vibration for the information that I have put in my first book. Once linked through at the vibration you have managed to harmonise with from your earthly form, much can be shown to you at other levels also. This is because it is easier to function and express yourself at these higher vibrations once you are removed from your material conditions and expression.

Crystal spheres

You are beginning to make your first links to the crystal spheres of life at this stage, which are the next spheres after the ones linked to earth by the colours. This is because all life is a gradual progression and blending. Colours are used still, of course, in these spheres of life, but with more expansion of hues and concentration through the crystal vibration. I had my first introduction to this when I was shown my correct attunement to the green vibration. (At last!)

I was walking through life and taking out of the gutters by the side of the road a collection of items that had been discarded by others. When I reached the end of my journey I found I was at the seashore. In my hand, instead of the bits and pieces I had been carrying I held a beautiful large green crystal.

I asked what to do with this and then saw a Buddha-like statue, although I knew it was representative of religion as a whole. The location of the "third eye" on the statue was empty and I knew I had to place my crystal there.

I was warned to turn away immediately because of the light. Golden light streamed from the statue, past where I then stood looking out to sea, and lit up all the land.

Blue stairs

When I had continued my earthly life experiences for some years, during which many parts of my life had altered, I continued with my journey up the staircase. I was determined to take great care with the blue vibration and proceed slowly so that I only had to do it once!

These stairs brings you to another landing, of course, and this time I found that there was a clear view of the earth at this level. This was not possible in the same way from the green vibration, as you are still linked in to the earth, as shown in the picture of the pathway leading to the seashore of physical life described above. There were various doorways at this level where different people who belonged to this colour, lived. So it becomes very clear that once you have reached this stage of spiritual progression and understanding, you are being gradually removed from a material existence, and the pathway has lead you onto the spiritual dimensions of life.

There is, of course, a great deal to learn once more, as you have a new vista on the world, and I have noticed quite a few differences in my spiritual techniques and experiences as I am trying to work from this vibration. One of the earliest experiences I remember happened when I had an astral experience while my body was asleep.

I was travelling with spirit helpers to give urgent assistance some distance away, and I was aware that this was the first time I had been able to be included. We were propelling ourselves through the beautiful blue sky and passing the clouds. I could not resist playing on a cloud, as I had always wanted to do this, and was quickly hurried along, "We don't have time for that!"

I have also become aware, for example, that mental healing for the world can be projected by visualising yourself in a position in the atmosphere, quite a way from the earth, and working from this position. The earth appears blue from here. At a personal level you are learning to fully grasp the meaning of self-control and patience, so that you do not speak in haste or anger whatever the circumstances. You have to learn not to react in fear or temper to the lack of self-control of others.

Effect on your relation to your chakras

The red and blue vibrations of your nature are blending and assisting one another, as the blue combines with the natural red of the base chakra. The strength of indigo is eventually mastered, and the final result is the true blending of the red of the base chakra with the blue to produce purple.

One of the important differences is an adjustment to the relation of colour to all your chakra energy centres. Once you are learning to function at the blue vibration, it is helpful to imagine that you are standing on green, which can be visualised as grass. This is because you are now tuning into the blue vibration in your life, and can visualise your link to the green vibration through the soles of your feet.

This means that your base chakra should be visualised as blue, the sacral as purple, the solar plexus as white, the heart chakra as silver and the throat as gold. The gold links through to the area of the "third eye", which should now be developing into fourth, fifth and sixth going up the forehead, giving expanded spiritual visions and astral experiences. The crown chakra will be linking to the crystal vibration as you progress, with all the colours in an arc around the head. This is a visualisation and indication of the progress you will be making later.

Then you are ready to progress onwards once more, with the blue vibration at your feet, and purple as the vibration at the base chakra. When the purple vibration has been learnt and understood and can be used properly the person is no longer linking to the earth, or the astral spheres belonging to the physical, to function. The last colour realm relating to the earth is purple, and you are now ready to enter the white vibration where all colours are used in their correct way and correct blending.

Choices on the way

It must be stressed, as always, that your speed of progress is individual and you will also have many choices along the way. Free will is always in operation, and, although our free will is limited, we always have plenty of choices in our lives. Your choices may affect the speed of your progress, but it is always important to feel you are happy and ready to experience another part of your journey.

An example of choosing your own direction is a choice I made as I was attempting to attune correctly to the green emotional vibration (although I did not realise this at the time.) I had been studying yoga for some time, and learning to meditate. Astral travelling was discussed at my yoga class, and several members expressed an interest in travelling the world at the astral level, jokingly observing it would save a lot of money normally spent on holidays! As I was listening to them the thought consolidated in my mind that I was not interested in travelling at the earthly level, as this could be achieved by normal physical means. I asked to travel upwards, to see the spheres of life beyond the physical, if possible, whilst I still possessed a physical body. The more I thought about it the more that seemed a much better option for astral travelling, and I became set on the idea.

This occurred in the mid-1980s and my busy life continued, during which I learnt much more about spirituality and meditation, and experienced life-changing episodes in my everyday life. It was some ten years later that I reached the stage of development and understanding to begin to experience the astral travelling described in my first book. My request had been answered: I had received all the tuition and experiences needed, and was most privileged to remember my astral visits to the spheres.

Patience

Any requests we make do take time to bring into being, whether for material events or progression, or spiritual development. We often assume nothing is happening because we are not aware of what is being done on our behalf. It is important not to give up because spiritual progress especially can suddenly flower when least expected.

It cannot be stressed enough that it never works to try to rush spiritual progress. As I was working hard to learn as much as I could and help people, I learnt about the raising of the red vibration up the spine to blend with the blue. When done at the correct time and when you are completely ready to make this blending it, of course, gives you the purple vibration that is often associated with true spirituality. I know, however, from personal experience that this should never be attempted too soon, as you are dealing with the powerful creative red energy of the life force. This is the procreative energy force attracting male and female, and should only be brought into use on the vibration of true love, or not at all, as it can otherwise be very disruptive. Fortunately it can be returned to the base of the spine and the slower, steady progress continued.

In fact when I was shown this stage recently it was achieved by taking the purified and balanced blue vibration down the body to the red, and then bringing the purple that was thus created up the body cleansing all the chakras on the way.

Freedom and Spiritual Law

So we return to the concept of freedom and we can see by the stages discussed so far that we gain true freedom by control of self—stage by stage—and are set free from our lower self, our appetites, desires, and self-interest. Freedom is gained not by avoiding and running away from problems but by facing responsibilities and decisions and dealing with them. We also have to realise that our actions affect other people. We have to face and accept the law of cause and effect at the spiritual level, as mentioned at the beginning of the book. We have free will but what we do will always have consequences, some good and some, perhaps, not so good.

The finer consequences of thought and action, the non-physical consequences have to be understood and taken into account. The emotional hurt to others, for example, which delays their progress, is not linked into the physical concept of time in the same way as the purely physical law of cause and effect as seen in physical objects. Indeed, it can take a lifetime or several lifetimes before the consequences of past actions come into play at the physical level.

We can say that the law of cause and effect is the physical aspect of a spiritual law that as you give out at a certain vibration of life so you will receive at that vibration. "As you give so you receive," or sometimes referred to as "karma." So there is compensation and retribution here and hereafter, depending on your vibration. Life is continual progression, and we learn from our experiences or "mistakes" of life.

Our most difficult experiences are often the most helpful to us in the long term, as they show us our nature, our weaknesses but also our strengths. We find we are with a certain group of people, our family or friends, for much of our life. This is for a reason, it is to work out the relationships to help and understand past and present events. When the balance is reached the relationships may no longer be relevant, or may continue because we wish to help one another in the "freedom" of the future.

Progress

To progress you have to learn to leave part of yourself behind, not just the people you used to know and the place in which you used to be. If you are still linked in your mind then you have not moved at all. You cannot change your life by moving house and suchlike if you have not altered. You have to alter yourself and give up the way you were: strive to become a different person in some way, to behave in a new way. Then your life will change and the way others react to you in the future will change also. Leaving the old you behind is not at all easy. It entails learning the lessons of what happened before, to truly discover what made you wish to alter your life.

You need to see yourself as you really are in order to be able to activate this process. This perception can be given to you from spirit, often when you have reached a major point of decision in your life. In my experience you are very surprised to discover where you have been in error. When I had finished one phase of my life and knew large changes were unavoidable, I found myself reviewing my life and my opinion of my past actions. My guides came close and discounted many of my "mistakes" as learning experiences.

What I had considered my best attribute they informed me was where I had in fact erred. To my surprise I was informed that I had been far too "soft" with people up to then, which had not helped them or me, as I had given them the impression that it was in order to treat people badly by accepting their behaviour towards me.

I knew I must slowly learn to correct this attitude and have spent many hard years since trying to get it right! However, your nature needs to be in balance if you wish to lead a spiritual life and spend the bulk of your time in spiritual activity, so all the hard slow progress is always worth it. Part of this process involved learning to let go of other people and learning not to try to control their lives.

We often unconsciously try to influence others and are afraid of losing people if they make life choices that worry us. As in all spiritual matters, the opposite applies, and we keep their love by granting them their free will and "letting them go."

Interestingly, I became aware of a physical problem with possible arthritis in the joints of my fingers at this time. I could not understand why this condition was developing. It was explained to me by spirit that trying to 'hold on' to people in my life, and worrying about their behaviour, I was causing this condition in my hands. My body was trying to tell me to let go by making it physically difficult tfor me to hold onto objects. It was further explained to me that each digit represented a relationship, females linking to the left hand and males to the right. The thumbs are mother and father or husband or wife, depending on your present life circumstances. The first finger relates to the oldest child, the second finger to the next oldest and so on. If you have no children of your own, these can relate to brothers and sisters, or children to whom you are emotionally attached. I was told to very gently massage the joints, asking for healing, and mentally releasing the person and the worry I was feeling. I did this and slowly the joints returned to normal.

Healing

In this and many other ways, which will vary from person to person, we learn to work on ourselves until our emotional balance and control is achieved. The person has to be whole, balanced and harmonised to go further into a spiritual existence. We can become very lop-sided in our mental and emotional nature if we have several distasteful experiences from males or females, developing a fear and bias against one sex. Our own nature has two sides to it, the active and passive perhaps being one of the best descriptions of this duality. Therefore our attitude to others has to be cleansed and harmonised and our fears healed before we can progress to another stage of our development.

The chakras or energy centres of our being need to be cleansed, and the two sides of our mind and emotions, represented by the two sides of our physical body, balanced and active. We cannot move on to a larger expression of our reality if unresolved problems or untreated damage exist in our present reality. We have to be able to express our whole being, without fear, in our life as it is at the moment in order to be satisfied with ourselves. We are then able to leave this stage behind and learn to experience a more extended and fuller life.

Trust

Trust your instinct and your reason
For together they combine
Lift your heart and mind together
Upwards to the Love Divine

All the universe around us
Speaks of balance and "the whole"
We need all our dual nature
To reach our precious, heavenly goal

The peace of God is there within us
Strength and comfort from above
Leave a moment in the bustle
To receive the Heavenly Love.

The next stage

So we have progressed and are reaching the stage of wishing to lead a spiritual life whilst still living in the world. We have to learn to turn this difficult concept from theory into practice. I had a discussion about this with my sister, who, like my brother, is older than I am! She quoted a saying to me that she had found most helpful in understanding how to do this:

*"To live the spiritual life and tread the spiritual pathway you have to learn the art of being **in** the world but not **of** the world."*

The body of course will always consist of earthly components, but you choose the vibration for your mind, and consequently, your thoughts and deeds. The body can become "the temple of the spirit," and the physical life lived by spiritual values. You come to the realisation that your various bodies are coats that can be taken off. Your reality is not dependent on whether you have a physical or other coat on—you are you with or without a physical body.

The reality of this truly comes to you when you leave the lower part of your self and progress onwards as your higher self from the temple on other side of the river.

The pathway was leading further away from the material life.

Chapter 5

Treading the pathway—"Be the Pathway"

TO be "in the world but not of the world" can be put another way. This other concept of the same idea was given to me when I visited a Spiritualist church looking for more guidance. The philosophy, which is given in the first part of the Sunday services, was on "Treading the Spiritual Pathway" and gave me the instruction I was seeking. The speaker was eloquently inspired from spirit, and explained that to tread the pathway you had to "Be the Pathway." I did not understand what this meant at all when I heard it, and had to think long and hard before I began to realise what you had to do.

"Be the Pathway"

You have to *make* the pathway for yourself; you have to wholly become an example of a spiritual person. You have to live the spiritual life, every day and not just sometimes. In your actions and your speech you have to strive for spiritual improvement. Once you have managed the process you will be able to assist others to make their own spiritual pathway. They will be able to follow your example but not tread your pathway. You are helped in the process by previous pioneers but each person has to follow their own pathway.

It has also to be your free choice to take this way, as it can only be made in truth and honesty. It will not happen if it is the will or wish of someone else.

You will find that your decisions in life will be taken from a different standpoint, and for spiritual reasons rather than material ones. You will pray for the guidance to choose aright and to give correct advice.

You will find you are not necessarily trying to assist others to gain material possessions, or even material positions or accolades. The importance of health, of peace of mind, of understanding and giving regard to others, and to having the time to appreciate the wonders of life, will become more and more apparent to you. The attractiveness of material, contrived pleasures will fade, and you will wish to lead a simpler, more natural life.

The realisation that you are an eternal being, and are only visiting the earth for a little while, will alter your priorities and change your attitude. The acquisition of spiritual gifts, to receive messages, to heal, to see and hear spirit and travel the other spheres of life will become the important goals.

This is only the beginning of your spiritual awakening, however, because, as it so correctly states in the Bible, these gifts are "as tinkling bells" if you have no love for your fellow humans. It is when you realise that love for others is the key to life that your pathway truly begins. Service is the password of the spirit, service to others. As you serve, so others will give service to you in true brotherly and sisterly love.

Because all life is ruled by perfect, natural, spiritual law, you will discover the truth that as you give, so you will receive. The vibrations you give to others will return to you. Your life will contain difficulties, but as you help others so the necessary assistance will come to you. Probably not from where you expect, and often not even from physical beings, but when you ask, the strength, the guidance and the assistance will come.

Spiritual training in your life experiences

The many experiences that we have gradually alter and extend our understanding of life, although we often do not understand the reason for them until later. There are many opportunities and relationships that we can easily see are part of the plan for our spiritual understanding and the growth of our nature. This is the positive side of the coin, so to speak. However, there are also experiences, especially the unpleasant ones, which we only comprehend in retrospect.

Then there is the other side of the coin altogether, where there are the checks and blocks we all encounter to our plans and attainments. It is puzzling and annoying to find that we are not able to pursue a talent, for example, that we can, and wish, to express. Sometimes the revenue is not available, or circumstances beyond our control make it impossible for us to continue. It is understandable that we are often drawn to occupations and expressions of our abilities from previous times. However, if we are to expand and develop ourselves, these accomplishments need to be remembered only, reawakened and used as part of the fabric of our new life. We should not be reliving the past, but using our progress so far to enable us to learn new skills and capabilities. This can be likened to a child learning to walk, and then extending this skill to running, and finally using these skills to reach a destination or person.

So, often the blocking of an easy pathway for us leads to far greater development and progress for us in the long term. As we have said, spiritual progress is permanent and an eternal journey, and therefore, easy routes in fact, slow the process down.

The truth of the matter is that we make some decisions about our lives before we come, although generally do not retain much memory of these decisions. I am sure I speak for most of us when I say that there are many parts of my life that were best dealt with as they happened. Prior knowledge would have been no help. So the pattern is laid for us with our agreement, but obviously with our free will as the controlling factor at our command.

Our conscience is our guide and is the sum total of our learning up to the present, and acts as our natural pathfinder. This we can rely on as our natural link with our higher intention, whether we have received any other messages of guidance or not. When the person involved agrees to aim for spiritual progress in life, circumstances will occur to provide the lessons needed, and also the opportunities for growth.

The progress of the spirit is continual and, as mentioned earlier, we learn to pass on our knowledge and understanding to others when we are ready to do so. This does not have to be as a teacher in the strict sense of the word, but as your spiritual progression occurs your behaviour and actions react on others to assist them as a natural process. The whole process of your spiritual development will culminate in you becoming a whole, balanced spirit, able to use your more refined bodies to correctly control the physical. You are enabled to pass through from the spiritual life to the physical world the spiritual gifts of healing, guidance, and assistance to others, in service.

The progression is from a created being, able to express natural talents, to a creative spirit, able to assist the life force in directing the energy of life, creating happier people, with optimism for the future and an understanding that life is eternal. As you look back at your life you will be able to see the reason and effect of the experiences that you did not understand at the time. You will have been brought to the point where you are ready and able to cope with spiritual work, possessing the compassion and understanding to truly assist with the difficulties of others. It is only when you experience something yourself that you truly understand how it feels, as personal experience is usually the best teacher of all.

How spiritual training happens

In my previous book the portals are described that link the physical life with the life in spirit, depicted in Chapter 2, called Transition. These portals are places of preparation and healing, and link to various spheres of spiritual life. They are the organised places for preparation and entry into the physical life, and for recuperation from the physical and preparation for entry into the spiritual life. The various pathways of life lead to the next levels of existence, as explained in my first book. People arrive at the top of the pathway leading from the physical life, after healing and adjustment as necessary in a portal, and go to greet their relatives and friends at the appropriate colour vibration of life.

Relationships

The departments of each portal serve as a demonstration of the different aspects and relationships of life we have to experience and understand before we become a complete and balanced spirit. We learn about each area and the different ways in which we can help others, firstly through the personal relationships in our lives. We relate personally to the portal departments in the following ways:

The departments that prepare people for entry into physical life represent the female relationships of our lives at the personal level. We have to fully understand and relate properly to the mother, sister and daughter relationships. This means that we have to function properly as each of these ourselves or relate properly to others in these roles in respect to us.

The departments that heal people of physical problems and prepare them for entry into their spiritual life represent the male relationships of our lives at the personal level. Once more, we have to understand and relate properly to the father, brother and son relationships in the same manner. We may find in our lives that we have to take the role of father to our children for a while, for example, even though we are female, or vice versa, which brings us the understanding of the difference of the other role. It is not necessary to live a whole life in each of these roles, just have enough of the experience to understand and relate to each relationship in the correct way.

The husband/wife relationship is truly successful when all the other relationships are understood. You are then ready to learn to become a father and mother together, capable of expressing love to each other in whatever way it is needed. We often say that when we find a true partner in life they fulfil our needs in every way. When you have found your true partner you are both then also capable of giving to those you help the assistance they require. This is shown in the portal as the father/mother soul who assists all the work of the portal, linking in from the white sphere of spiritual life. When we have successfully understood this relationship we will have completed all the aspects of personal life represented by the portal.

Training in each transition department

The person learns to express themselves in service in each of the departments, with experiences in the physical world and in the spiritual worlds or spheres that correspond to the different departments. This learning process is not restricted to the physical vibration. We have experiences when we are asleep which complement our daily lives, and assist us to learn, even though these are not generally remembered. However, we often find that sleeping on a problem will bring a fresh approach. As we begin to establish contact with our spiritual helpers we can bring the awareness of the ongoing help we are given into our physical consciousness.

This serves to quicken our progress as we can learn to receive thoughts and assistance through symbols, as discussed earlier, to guide us.

When the physical life is finished, the person will take up the spiritual work of the department, interacting with the physical world, until more earthly experience is needed. We learn how to train souls for the physical life, depending on their progression and understanding and the life they have to lead. We also learn how to heal people in the portal to enable them to continue their life in spirit.

When all the departments have been experienced and the lessons learned, the person has become a whole spirit as regards the vibrations of life in relation to the physical. The person has become able to express and harmonise all the colours and can now function as a "white" soul, as one half of a father/mother combination, to assist and organise a portal and all the departments.

Other training in spirit

This is an example of how progression is made and there is much other work that is undertaken apart from, but in harmony with, this assistance given to spirits to enter and leave the earthly life. But it serves to demonstrate the basis of the understanding and skills that must be learned before we can progress enough to work completely on the spiritual vibrations of life, rather than the physical and spiritual combined.

Some of the other work involves assisting people to cope with their life on the earth, and indeed, training to become an inspirer or guide by observation from the spiritual side of the operation. Other work is specialised, such as trying to rescue souls who dwell in the darker places on the spiritual side of life, who can see no light. Great and persistent effort is made by dedicated souls who plumb these depths to shine their light until some response eventually comes from the minds of these trapped and despairing people. This work, especially, is always done under strong protection and in groups, never alone.

People living in spirit obviously have their own private lives to lead, hobbies, families and recreation as well as their work, and all is organised in co-operation. Because energy is generally absorbed straight from nature in the spiritual spheres, much of the effort that is needed in the physical world to sustain the body is not necessary, and therefore a much freer life is possible.

Work in spirit as well as on earth

When you have progressed to the stage of working in spirit when you are asleep as well as in your physical life, your spiritual training has obviously entered another stage. You are becoming a spirit working on the earth, possessing a physical body, and the spiritual eternal realities of life are the important and guiding principles that govern your behaviour.

You can be aware of this work, or just aware that you are tired when you wake as if you have been working all night. The amount of recollection varies, but one can ask to have this ability awakened. You must take into account, however, that the accuracy will vary because of the difference in vibration. The other factor to be taken into account is that you will then carry these experiences with you as part of your mind in your daily life and will be beginning to live beyond the three-dimensional reality. This does, obviously, take some adjusting to, and entails creating quiet times in your schedule to retune your mind from one vibration to another.

Mind techniques

It is necessary to learn some basic techniques of the mind, to be able to envisage a mental shield of golden shimmering light around oneself, for example, as a protection before entering the workaday world. The different doors to the various compartments of the mind have to be controlled, so that you can tune yourself to the different vibrations of everyday life and spiritual life as necessary. This is not easy and meditation helps a great deal as you learn to calm the functioning of the mind, and control the emotions. It is most important not to become overtired as it is easy to forget that mental and emotional exhaustion can be more damaging to your functioning as a person than physical exhaustion.

Merging

This work merges into one as you progress, because all life is one, and you become used to moving from one vibration to another. You may have recollections of being with people you know on earth working in a spiritual place, and visions of people who are now in spirit being with you in a physical location. I find myself speaking to my parents at times, when the physical body is asleep, in their living room as it was when they were alive. There was much spiritual activity here in their lifetimes and that gives it a spiritual reality to be used as a meeting place.

Healing—of others

When this stage of spiritual progression is reached you will find that you are involved in the healing of other people as a natural part of your life. This is not necessarily as a "spiritual healer," but can be done in your daily work, or you will find that you are always listening and trying to help others with their problems. So the healing process has naturally gone beyond the correction of your own imbalances, although this still occurs. You will have a continual involvement and compassion for others, and are learning how to be a healing spiritual energy, drawing from the creative source of life to assist.

It is necessary to master the technique of keeping your own vibration positive and optimistic when helping others. This is so that you do not let your own energy be drained by joining the person in their negativity. Because you keep yourself in tune with the positive life force, you can draw upon the continual power of the Creator to send energy to the person who needs it. This is a difficult state to achieve as compassion pulls you to the other person's vibration, and their experiences can trigger memories of your own.

You will need healing for yourself also, and must watch for emotional exhaustion as mentioned before. When a healing treatment is conducted correctly the healers should feel better as well as the patient, as the healing energy will pass through the healers benefiting them also.

We should now be realising that healing is really of the spirit, which permeates to the mind and body, and can bring results that can be much quicker and more effective than by bodily means alone. It is a question of learning to accept the reality of what we would call miracles in the everyday sense. To witness and believe the truth that spiritual law can override the material laws of life and produce physical results that seem impossible and have no physical explanation. The healing done by my husband and myself over the years have shown this to us.

We have also realised that all spiritual work is really one, and the healing process is achieved as much by the messages given from spirit, healing the mind and emotions, as by the direct treatment with spiritual energy.

Healing—for yourself

You have come to the point of realignment so that your spiritual bodies can function harmoniously through the physical, enabling you to be a spiritual being working on the physical vibration. Your chakra energy centres need to be cleansed of hurt and the blockage caused by traumas. The vibrations relating to the physical life, represented by the colours, need to be linked to the spiritual vibrations, which are quicker and stronger. A channel is thus provided through from the higher spheres for you to use, so that your physical being and mind is gradually brought under the control of your higher self. You are still yourself but will find that you can look back and see that many of the characteristics that made up your individuality have changed.

This is a disrupting and tiring process and is managed for you by spirit, either through healers in the body or directly by your spiritual helpers. Personally I experienced a combination of healing from others, instructions from spirit to assist them to cleanse and heal myself whilst conscious, and healing experiences on the astral spheres when asleep. The chains that tie you to the physical world are being removed, so that you are no longer held by your own previous actions and experiences, or those of others.

The perceptions that the reality of the world is fleeting and restricted, and that you can experience other vibrations of life whilst possessing a physical body, are now progressing from a theoretical understanding to a practical reality.

Each energy centre of the body has to be cleansed, healed and balanced, and each one brought under the control of the mind, so that the person can direct the energy flow as they wish. Healing of the emotions occurs for each energy centre. At the blue vibration, relating to the throat area chakra, for example, the mental experience of loss and sorrow is healed, as blue deals with the emotional content of the mind. There is a link with symbols here once more, as we learn to accept that in the reality of the spiritual life sorrow at the loss of a loved one is unreal.

However, we can only accept the truth of this when we can tune in to the vibrations of life other than the physical and so link again with people who no longer possess the physical body. Whilst we think of them as "dead" and believe that we are separated from them, this linking is made difficult, and the healing of the grief is made difficult also.

The purple vibration—going beyond the blue

When we are ready to be released from this trauma deep blue and red are used for the necessary strength and energy. The tears and tension held in the solar plexus have to be released and the blockage at the neck of unvoiced suffering. Grey colour is breathed out as all this is released, and then the head cleared, through a head massage, with a grey mist issuing from the mouth. It is helpful if this occurs in water, in the bath for example, as water is used as a cleanser, and can be then flushed away. The deep blue then has free passage to travel down to the base chakra to form purple and come back up the body cleansing the navel chakra and expelling all the grey suffering down and out of the body. This turns red as it is expelled, followed by white to heal all three chakras, the solar plexus, the sacral and the base.

Once the three lower chakras are functioning properly, spiritually speaking, and the heart chakra is tuned in to love in service, the throat, brow and crown chakras can be attuned also. The purple colour ascends, attuning the top half of the body before it reaches the crown chakra, and the process is completed.

The awareness of the person is now ready to progress once more to learn about the white vibration of spiritual life. Progress has been from a material existence through a gradual process to an existence based on spiritual values and using the vibrations of life, illustrated by the colours, at a spiritual level. The actions and reactions of the person will now be spiritually based and the vibrations of life they use will be seen in their aura, or energy field, as spiritual colours rather than physical hues.

The pathway is leaving the physical world, and the view of the world will become further and further away.

Chapter 6

Leaving the Physical Vibration

The white vibration

THIS vibration contains all the colours, in the same way as white light contains all the colours of the rainbow. The square of physical life is being left behind and you are learning to centre your mind at the spiritual vibration. Each type of person and colour vibration has been experienced and understood. The lesson of loving people as they are, no matter how they look at life, has to be put into practice. It is extremely difficult to send the love vibration to others when they have hurt you badly, or have behaved in a terrible way, but it is the only way to truly help them.

You will experience the speeding up of the law of action and reaction—you will find your outgoing vibration returning to you more and more quickly. Instead of having to wait until the end of a lifetime to review your progress, you will receive interim reports, then periodic reviews as dreams, progressing to daily assessments and finally continual contact with your guiding influences to monitor and encourage you in your pathway.

Thus you will receive the assistance you require to begin to live in this new way, and you must always ask for the help you need, as it is a very large adjustment. Do not worry about finding it almost impossible, failing often, and backtracking also. This is all part of the process, but you can begin anew each day.

You will experience depression, entering the darkness of loneliness and despair in order to find the light. The events of your life will probably tax you to the utmost, but you must not give up as it is the last part of this long journey of experience and will be well worth it when you emerge into the light of eternal spiritual life.

Forgive as you go

You have to learn to forgive as you go, others and yourself, first forgiving all past hurt, and then present day problems. This forgiveness releases you from the pain and also the other people. The task then is to try to forgive people automatically as they injure you, working on the vibration of mother/father love. You forgive them as you would your own child, but realising that you have hurt many people yourself also, and must not judge.

Healing yourself—cleansing

Water is used as a cleanser for this process, to release you from one vibration to another, releasing the pain from inside. The bath is used to do this work, and the water flushed away immediately. Hurt from males is registered on the right side, and female on the left side. The pain has to be acknowledged and released, linking with various incidents and people and various parts of the body, including tension in the head which will need to be massaged away.

Where you are on the pathway

You make your own future as you go now; your own effort is deciding your progress. The green door, at the top of the green stairs, will be able to be closed behind you and you will find that the golden ball of the handle will come off in your hand for you to carry with you. The blue door is closed in the same way, with deep grief at the separation from the people who wish to stay at this vibration. This golden ball handle will stay in your other hand, and you hold one in each hand to use as your imprint to make your own footsteps on the first step of the white stairway.

Climbing the white steps

Making your own footsteps—a spiritual creation

This process occurs in meditation and in sleep state. The golden power that issues from the Source, the creative power of life or God has to be linked with before you can begin. You will be standing on a landing with the steps in front of you. Your hands are held up with the arms extended and this stream of power is visualised as pouring into your hands and head.

The power is then used flowing out the other way through fingertips one by one by placing the hands on the first step. You use your hands to make a shape for you to step onto when completed, turning it into a footprint. You are climbing Jacob's ladder!

The fingers and thumb make the marks month by month, with the hands facing one another, first the left hand, then the middle bar of gold, and then the right hand. The little finger is at the top and this golden line is made first, flowing in a continual stream down the arm until the line is complete. You start with your birthday month, and each finger is used for a month.

So the five fingers of the left hand make their marks as you go through the year, sometimes spirit instructing you to do a month right at the beginning, sometimes in stages as you go through the month. This will depend on what problems you are facing, and how active your physical life is in that month.

When the first half is finished you are shown that a cross is being made on the body shape, the top of the cross is going up through the head and down the body, the shoulders making the crossbar. This links the whole body through to the shape you are forming in order for you to be able to step up onto the shape made at the end of the process.

When you reach the sixth month you form the central bar, imagining the golden power flowing down your spine and linking with the shape where the ends of all the lines from the left are thus joined in the middle. The fingers and thumb of the right hand are used for the next five months, linking from the right to the left, attaching them to the central bar.

In the last month the completed shape is linked to the source and to yourself with no loose ends, the outside edges of the lines being joined up also. You step up onto the shape and stand in your birthday month.

The process is very hard with blockages on the way; you come across experiences you would rather forget and have to forgive yourself and others. There is mental and emotional pain. However, your complete body is now harmonised with the next level of your life.

The light from the footsteps of previous travellers has blended together to form the steps for you, and you add your vibration for the future. In this way we assist one another, although we have to make the individual effort ourselves.

There is much help and encouragement from loved ones who wish to see you progress, forming a continual instruction throughout the process.

The next steps

So you have completed one step, and in order to progress any further, you must, of course, start the process all over again. A process can occur, once more with the aid of water in the bath, when you have reached this first step. The hands and feet are held up together into the air, with the body in the water as a conductor, and the thus the link to spirit is made for the feet to travel onwards and upwards. The golden stream of power enters the hands and feet and down into the body.

You do not have to be afraid to climb further. There now may be an image shown to you of a ladder in sections, which can flip up or down. This is used by spirit to visit the earthly vibrations. But now you wish to climb, so, even if you temporarily flip the ladder back down, you can return and continue your climb. You need to imagine depth to each step, turning the ladder into steps, which will assist the next person who climbs.

You are learning the lessons of the white vibration, tuning into the spiritual vibration of all the colours and improving your behaviour. You will be able to access the white vibration of spiritual life, although you may not remember it, where there is a "wardrobe" of coloured garments for you to choose, depending on the spiritual work being accomplished.

The pathway has left the square of physical life behind. The next shape to be encountered will be the triangle of spiritual life, which will be explained later in this chapter.

Progress review

So the process follows this pattern. The colours of life are understood on a spiritual rather than a physical vibration, and are used correctly, bringing the person to the white vibration of life, which is the top sphere relating to the physical life. Once the purple vibration is attuned to, the chakras can be linked to a correct and true spiritual use, and the white door of spiritual life can be opened. This white sphere of life gives entry to the first golden sphere, the golden gates that people refer to as heaven. There is much to be learned here, and the white body, that encompasses all colour vibrations correctly, is used.

Through the golden gates

Thereafter there is much tuition at this level of spiritual life. The colours of life have to be understood as a spiritual vibration, where their intensity, range and use are greatly extended. This does not mean that you cannot possess a physical body and continue to live on the earth, but, obviously, your life will not be lived in the same way as you progress.

I described the room that I was shown at this level of spiritual life in "Wish You Were Here?" when explaining about the healing process at different stages of spiritual existence. (Chapter 4, "Spiritual Healing, Healing from Sphere 11.")

I also made reference on the last page of that book to a vessel of pure fire in this room, into which we leap to be purified, and lose the dross of our physical existence.

The elements of life—going from white to crystal energy rays

You are in fact trained to use all the elements of water, fire, earth and air to heal and to create. These become your tools of creation once you have understood the purpose and functioning of each element.

Water relates to the emotions, and this is why we can go past the waterfall from the material life on a vibration of true love.

Fire is used to cleanse, and also to break down created forms into the basic components. The flame produced is a pure flame of energy that is released. We can see this in candles, coal fires and so on at the physical level. It is used in the same way at the spiritual level.

The air element is used by spiritual beings in a personal way as you learn to fly, which is a normal method of movement in the astral planes. The breath of life is also the way that energy is imbibed in a spiritual life, once the stage of wishing to eat and drink has passed.

You have to progress beyond these abilities, from using the white vibration for expression, encompassing all the colours, to a crystal vibration.

The earth element is linked to through rock and crystal: this is the spiritual foundation and link for earth. Crystals are energy transmitters at the physical level, being used for this purpose in radios, computers and so on. Crystals therefore can be used in the same way in the healing process and the physical body has a small crystal inside the skull.

The crystal spheres of life are the next phase of life in spirit, and using spiritual energy through a crystal body is the next process of spiritual life. The rays of colour are used to transmit energy, using the spiritual range of colours rather than the ones that directly link with the physical vibration.

This crystal vibration, which feeds energy to the earth from a higher level, is learned step by step, so that the transition is a gradual one, following on from learning the use of colours in the spiritual spheres.

Crystal colours are beamed towards the earth, linking through the colour vibrations used at the slower vibrations, increasing the intensity of the energy through the prism of crystals, rather than just a colour vibration. These vibrations are used in the crystal spheres themselves also to activate life there and communicate.

You progress using the crystal vibration instead of the white vibration for expression, learning to use the different colour rays then combining them as their working crystal shape grows. This is briefly explained in my previous book in Chapter 3, "Spheres of Life Beyond the Physical World, Sphere 13 and Beyond."

When all these skills have been learned you can still link back to the white realm at the top of the astral planes belonging to the earth. The wardrobe of clothes, however, will now be crystal, a shimmering display of sparkling colour.

Crystal triangles—going beyond the square of the physical

The square of human existence has to be satisfactorily completed before the triangular shapes of crystal expression can be experienced. The triangle is placed on top of the square, so to speak, as illustrated in the pyramids built by various civilisations to show this progression of the soul.

Two triangles are used, that make up a square, to bring energy to material vibration. This relates to the crystal vibrations of spiritual life, as there are more facets making triangles at the higher vibrations of the crystal levels of spiritual existence. This forms crystal shapes of increasing size as the person learns to use each new facet of crystal expression. Thus energy is brought from the crystal vibrations down into the material from one dimension to another. (This is explained further in *"Wish You Were Here?" Chapter 3, "Sphere 13 and Beyond."*)

Method

The triangles are used in the following way, once you have progressed successfully beyond the square of earthly experience. The two triangles are positioned one above the other. The first triangle is in the head, with the base between ears and the point above the head. You will find that this then rises above the head and spins to left (anti-clockwise) and there is a flashing of many lifetimes—all past physical lives.

You then have to rise and stand on top of this triangle, and you find you are standing in the second higher triangle. This also rises above the head and spins to the right (clockwise) for the future—your crystal life experiences.

You find yourself within the shape once more but it is now a large many-sided crystal. The crystal body is solidified emotion and you learn to control and understand emotion on the vibration of each colour in turn. One of the most important lessons is learning to maintain your own vibration of positive energy and love whilst helping others, no matter how deeply you commiserate with them. You have to learn to release yourself from your own fears, and then not allow yourself to be drawn into the fears and misunderstandings of others.

You have to hold your own position in faith and love to help them to change.

This applies to all situations and circumstances of life, not just when you are involved in giving healing to other people. This is energy control at its most delicate, and governs emotions linked to the mind and thought and pure vibrational energy.

This is how you bring the triangle of clear energy from spirit to the square of physical life, in order to raise others to a spiritual vibration. The possibilities of spiritual existence are endless, and the realisation of the reality of this expanded consciousness as a personal experience for yourself and others is the task given to you.

Leaving the crystal vibration

This is one of the most difficult vibrations to release as the crystal has to become liquid. You have learned to live in a crystal sphere of life, and you have to learn to rise above it into the clear blue sky beyond. The watery liquefied crystal is only a reflection of the sky. This process is done in meditation with the guidance and assistance of spirit as you have to live through the feeling of losing your true love, with the sensation of drowning.

You find you are holding the golden cord of life with which you are pulled out of the "water" into the reality of everlasting life. You are left holding this golden cord of life, and you need nothing else. You become a golden flame of energy and go into the sun of life. Then you are able to let go of the cord and just become part of the sun. You have let go of all the ties to the earth and are free to breathe the breath of life—spiritual life.

You have risen above the crystal world, and you can look back at the scenes within the crystal world. This works in exactly the same way as you viewed the scenes of the physical world from the blue vibration, and the higher view of the physical world that can be seen from the room used for healing at the white vibration of life through the golden gates of heaven.

The crystal world of expression has been yet another layer to be peeled off the inner being and then the larger, warmer, glowing power can be used. A step is taken nearer to unconditional love for all beings, projected from the soul without consideration of what will be returned. The golden love-stream from the creative power of life is felt, and the soul becomes a part of this stream of life, so that progression to the next stage of existence can occur.

The spirit blends with the golden light and becomes a free spirit.

The gold vibration—leaving the crystal

Expanding the consciousness further

Your awareness can now be attuned to the spiritual vibrations of life rather than the physical. You link to the colour vibrations as a channel for spiritual work and energy, instead of as a physical vibration for you to use for yourself and your own expression. The physical body is understood as the densest link in a chain of energy from the spiritual spheres to serve the creative force of life by supplying energy to others. Physical matter, the body in this case, is the servant of spirit, and the lessons to be learnt at this stage are how to control and channel energy on the love vibration to assist others.

You are tuned into a spiritual consciousness in the following way, in a state of meditation. The whole process is conducted by spirit and should not be attempted until a direction has come to you from spirit that it is time for this to happen. It should never be attempted otherwise.

It is not a quick process, but needs to be more or less continuous, and I was shown the stages over a fortnight. Before any work can commence there has to be an anchoring in the physical vibration. A rainbow of crystal is visualised at the feet, which keeps you attached through to the material world.

This process is going to take you beyond the crystal vibration, but you must be anchored there before any further progress can be made.

Attuning through the chakra centres

Then the chakras are attuned, beginning with the red of the base chakra, the male/female linking to provide the life energy for physical beings. This needs to have been cleansed, balanced and purified by the purple vibration. The sacral chakra links with children and the womb area, and this colour does not have to be too strong to function correctly, just as concentrated orange juice should not be drunk undiluted. The solar plexus is work in the world and as such should be a pure clear yellow.

Before the heart chakra is attuned a bath is needed to cleanse the system. The green of the heart chakra is difficult to attune as all selfishness has to be eliminated. The correct vibration of love for babies, children and young people has to be established, the willingness to help and teach them, fulfilling the responsibility for the start of the next generation.

The throat chakra attunement involves giving the power of speech over to the Life Force or God. You immerse in water to the top of the neck and visualise a tracheotomy, a hole into the throat to provide air. Your breath is to become the Breath of God, with no power of your own to be expressed, "Thine is the power." From now on all speech is for God. To prepare for this the arms and shoulders are lifted up to God and the golden healing power flows down the arms.

Then the throat is clasped and the breath held for a count of twenty, followed by a stretching out of the arms. A diamond of crystal is to be put in the third eye.

A golden chair

At this point the awareness comes that you are seated on a golden chair, located in the white healing room through the golden gates mentioned earlier. The eyes need to be closed as the crystal is placed in the third eye—there is no looking back, and the attunement occurs as you count to thirty, three times. There is entry into spiritual life and awareness now, and progression away from the square of physical life to a golden triangle shape. When the second count of thirty is reached the white steps are climbed.

The indigo of the third eye chakra has now been attuned and the purple vibration of the crown chakra needs to be cleansed. This happens in sleep state where a spirit 'hospital' is visited and all the colour clothing, including purple, is removed, and the body washed. You are cleansed of all emotional hurt from physical lifetimes. There is now the sensation of having the head replaced with a new one, changing your previous understanding of life coloured by personal emotions, to one of clear unbiased comprehension. This is a full reaping of the positive result of life's many experiences, with the negative emotional memories cleansed away. The purple colour vibration can travel up through the head giving a light-headed feeling. Spiritual hearing and vision will then begin to develop. You are now attuned to a spiritual vibration and can commence the pathway to spiritual life.

Adjustment to the new head has now to be accomplished. Healing is necessary from a healer to wake up the new head. The white lotus opens now on the top of the head as the crown chakra and under healing it explodes open in a rainbow of colour. Service has to be performed, in meditation, such as the symbolic washing of the feet of an enlightened spiritual helper. Their feet become those of people who need to be cleansed from your own personal life and then a person from your time who has been a negative influence in the world.

Your forgiveness and willingness to cleanse them opens up the white vibrational door for you.

The last stages

There is a barrier, represented by a brick wall, between you and the spiritual life. The mind has to be used from top to bottom, using light and whatever colour vibration is effective until the blockage has disappeared. Then a final cleansing is needed, a visualisation of a waterfall in a familiar scene in nature from your physical life. Then you find that you are standing in a new open place so full of light that the senses are stunned temporarily.

The spirit helpers will instruct you to use all your senses from the feet up to acclimatise yourself to the new vibration, using sight last. There is a sensation of being carried home. The pathway leads over the waterfall of true love and along the pathway on the other side of the river to the temple where the lower and higher selves meet.

When this is arrived at you become aware that you no longer have a lower body and are just light, and so can just ascend from the light base to the higher vibration. You have left the schoolhouse of life and passed from the playground, which is full of white light, dropping the physical body here and leaving it behind. An ascent is made past a schoolhouse vibration in spirit where spiritual work and adjustments have been made, to fly upwards into the spiritual life.

The next dimension

A golden cleansing now has to be performed, whilst a new white body is constructed which can be used for the link through from one vibration or dimension of spiritual life to another. There is a circle of light on the floor on which you have to stand for healing. Golden light streams up from this circle up through the body. The spiritual version of colours is used for the chakras: pink replaces red, peach replaces orange, lemon replaces yellow, lime for green and so on. The liquid golden light cleanses the dross from the person—the mistakes made at each level—and retunes them to a spiritual vibration.

There is a feeling of wing-like extensions at the back of the body and a rainbow around the head, an enlarged aura. You lift up when the process reaches the top of the body and feel able to fly. You then become aware that you are once again sitting on the golden chair but that the golden body has now been formed and is functional, and you can arise from the chair. There is a range of spiritual tools for you to use, that you will learn about next, and you take these with you into the next phase of spiritual life.

There is an explosion of energy, like water, but is, in fact liquid crystal, with eight droplets forming on the ends of the "spray." A creative vortex forms, appearing like a tunnel through which you could travel, from created form to the spiritual vibration of life where it is created.

The golden beam travels through the top of the head and out into a fan of seven antennae, with the middle splitting into gold and silver, and forming a crown shape. This explains the use of golden crowns in the physical world to denote leaders. You now have a complete gold functional body.

There is then a clockwise and anti-clockwise progression of energy through the body, with the golden thread of life blending with each chakra and colour. All the people ever encountered have to be forgiven, relating to each colour vibration. This thread comes out of the top of the head and you discover you are standing on the colour white. The new white body is being used, along with the gold one.

The white staircase—to go beyond the crystal

The white staircase, as described earlier, is before you in its entirety of thirteen steps, and the feet are bare. Gold and silver lights appear on the edges of each step as you go up them. At the top is an arc of colour from red through to white, with green in the middle. The silver and gold are two separate strands. You have to become the rainbow of colour and then blend the gold and silver together to become one strand. The last step appears as a large step and is very difficult to climb onto, as you are taking on work for the world and realise how difficult it will be. The crown is at the top and you can stand upright once more.

The golden triangle

The golden vibration of love has to be correctly attuned to and passed on. Where you have received a true love vibration in your life from someone close, you have to then pass this true vibration on by truly loving another.

This forms a golden triangle, from person to person, which is pathway you have to travel to go beyond the crystal vibration of life. The golden ring of the correct love vibration at the physical level, represented on earth by the wedding ring, is left on the chair. A large golden circle appears and you go through this circle, fastened onto the golden cord of life, to a crystal door. You go through the crystal door into a dark tunnel and come out into the light of another dimension of life.

You have progressed enough to travel onwards once more and are carried from top of the white staircase, where you now find yourself, to a beautiful resting place of intense pink. The other colours then appear around you.

You have risen above the crystal level, and find the body you now inhabit to be very light and supple, like a flame of light. The pathway leads on from here and you see the spiritual people with whom you link most closely. You pass through the circle of creation that is a swirling vortex, on your own colour vibration so that you can add your own colour to the other colours at this level of spiritual life. Life and healing at this stage of progression are covered in the next chapter.

The pathway has reached the realm of "Free Spirit."

Chapter 7

Life as a Free Spirit

THE pathway of life has now become a circular journey, a spiral of progress that travels smoothly upwards, with the square and triangle that relate to physical life and the astral planes being left behind. The dimensions have increased and will continue to increase, gradually progressing until the spirit lives in the reality of the oneness of life, and can see all dimensions from above as restrictions of the total reality.

The circle of life

The first stage of this new life is seen as a circle, with a cross in the middle, filling the circle. The numbers from one to twenty run round the edge of the circle, beginning at one just after where the cross meets the edge of the middle of the circle on the left.

Ten is opposite, where the cross meets the circle on the right, and eleven to twenty run around the bottom of the circle, with twenty ending up opposite ten. Progress has to be made around the circle, progressing from one number to another, and so from one sphere of life to another, just as progress was made around the square of physical life and around the triangle of spiritual ascension.

You are learning to apply all you have learnt in the lower spheres to this new vibration of life, which is the twentieth sphere. (This is explained in Chapter 3, "The Spheres of Life Beyond the Physical World," Spheres 20-27, of my previous book.)

Arriving

You arrive on the vortex of energy described at the end of Chapter 6, and find you are positioned in your own colour vibration at a point on the edge of the circle surrounding the vortex. The first action you have to take is to cross to the centre of this field of energy. There is a golden walkway that you cross and then you have to have confidence to hold the golden cord running through the middle of the vortex. You thus give your own creative colour to the mix for use in creation. This goes down to the physical level.

There is a circle of spiritual beings around the vortex who give of their own colour vibration to make the whole and much work is done co-operatively using the mix of colour vibrations as required. You can walk along the golden beam to the centre from your own colour to do your spiritual work—for yourself or for others whom you have brought to the circle to help them.

Healing at a higher level

A person is brought to this sphere of spirit for healing by a helper, and is held in the centre of the vortex of power on the golden thread of life. The work is done in an anti-clockwise direction, from the head to the feet. When the person is being awakened at this level they appear as a mist, and power from the members of the circle of spiritual beings consolidates the mist into their form from the head down to the feet.

The helper, a member of the circle, descends to earth vibration on a golden stream of power to link this renewal and healing to the physical body of the person being healed. Here the motion of the action is reversed to go clockwise, and from the feet to the head. The spiritual colours are linked to the physical chakras during this process: pink, peach, lemon, lime, powder blue, mauve, and white which comes out of the top of the head like a lotus flower. The golden stream of power goes out of the middle of this flower to link back to spirit.

When working as a healer using power from this realm there is the awareness that the colours flow as powerful rays from each digit of the hands.

Doors—Looking back

The doorways of life, opening onto the various stages of existence, are threaded like pearls onto the continuous golden stream of power issuing from the creative power of the universe. It is possible to look back now at the progression made as the spirit is free from these layers that block and restrict expression. The spirit is now closer to pure energy.

The door for the physical realms can be seen as a wooden door, as it is the medium of wood and nature that channels the power of spirit into the world of matter. This is the creative vibration that brings life to the world.

The door for the next vibrations of existence is a door of white light, as the medium of light links to the quicker vibrations of the realm of thought and ethereal reality. Souls here can journey back through the wooden door or on to the crystal vibration. The white light body of the soul is used, which contains all the colours and facets of the soul to be expressed at this level.

The crystal door takes the soul to the world of experience where creative power is channelled as laser-like beams through the medium of the crystal body of the soul.

When the soul progresses beyond these doors they can be looked back at and seen as steps on a journey, restrictions to the freedom of the expression of the reality of the inner being. The soul gains more and more freedom as control of the matter of the different realms of being is achieved.

Conclusion

And so each person realises eventually what it truly means to be a "free sprit." Each layer of being has been released as your spiritual self slowly breaks the bonds of one functioning reality after another.

To leave behind the physical life is truly the beginning of this wonderful adventure into the reality of your true existence. It is the commencement of the development and expression of your inner capabilities, released from the restrictions of a three-dimensional environment, the limited repertoire of the physical body, and the constraints of time.

The outer layers have been discarded and the spirit can now progress on the spiral of life, beginning with circle described, which then begins to ascend slowly, taking you on to more dimensions. The spirit that you are can progress onwards and upwards through many spheres and wondrous lives. The various layers are cast off, as has been explained. You become resplendent as a light being radiating out the glory of your individual vibration in joy, service and compassion to benefit the universe.

Life

Life is a never-ending spiral
Spirals of the Milky Way
Spirals of your DNA
Inner, outer, each reflecting
Pattern, order, harmony

Then let us tread the pathway gladly
Try to ascend in harmony
See our spiral grow and lighten
As we onward, upward go

See the whole of life in glorious union
Join the triumph of creation
Grant, O God, that we may be
Examples of Thy unity.

We will go on from this point to realise that the soul identity itself is a restriction of our being, that our true reality can be larger and freer once again.

When all of this process had been explained to me, of the increasing growth and freedom of the soul and spirit of each person to this point, I asked my inspirers, "What happens next?"

(They are always telling me that I ask too many questions!)

And the answer?

"Then we can begin!. . . "